In God's *Time*

Betty B. Hilton

ISBN 978-1-68570-930-3 (paperback)
ISBN 978-1-68570-931-0 (digital)

Copyright © 2023 by Betty B. Hilton

All rights reserved. No part of this publication may be reproduced, distributed, or transmitted in any form or by any means, including photocopying, recording, or other electronic or mechanical methods without the prior written permission of the publisher. For permission requests, solicit the publisher via the address below.

Christian Faith Publishing
832 Park Avenue
Meadville, PA 16335
www.christianfaithpublishing.com

Printed in the United States of America

They are all assembled in the church, all the players that are still alive and a few extra. But I know one thing with all my heart. I am exactly where God wants me to be right now. All that was about to happen was God's handiwork; I knew it was all preordained by Him. I trusted my God completely and He gave me the desires of my heart.

Chapter 1

I stood in the fellowship hall of the church alone listening to the guest coming into the church and all the children getting ready to take their places. I was waiting for my cue to come out, all dressed and ready to walk down the aisle, remembering where it all started.

It was a hot June, Saturday afternoon. I was at the Red & White grocery store to get a Wink soda and a small bag of chips. I was not a chocolate kind of girl. I could take it or leave it; I liked salty things. All my family and friends ate candy bars covered in chocolate. After I found what I wanted, I went to find my friend, Mrs. Hilton. I always went to her register if she was working so I could say hello. Her register was open, so I handed her my drink and chips, and we started talking, and she asked me out of the blue, "Betty, have you met my son Roger?"

I replied, "No, ma'am." She turned toward the end of the register where this amazing redhead was standing, putting my chips into a small bag. He looked up and smiled; trust me I was a goner, head over heels in love, right there, right then. I was so glad I did my hair before I went to the store. I was always careful how I looked; you never knew in a small town who you would run into. He asked me if he could walk me outside.

I said, "Sure, it's a free country." After we got outside, he asked if he could call me and I said, "Sure, my number is 553-7897."

He replied, "I will call you as soon as I get home."

I told him that would be nice, and I would look forward to talking to him; then I left the store parking lot. I walked fast going home I wanted to be there when and if he called. I had butterflies in my stomach waiting for him to call. He did call after a while; it was not that long, but it felt like forever to me. He had the sexiest voice

I had ever heard, and as far as I was concerned, he was dreamy. He told me that he knew my brother Ken; they were both going to be seniors at Berkeley High School. He then told me I would be going to school with his brother Mark, who would be starting his freshman year at Goose Creek High School like me. We talked a long time getting to know each other. He told me about his parents, his siblings, and I did the same. We talked about school and what we were going to study the upcoming year, what our favorite classes were, and what he wanted to do after graduation. I tell you, I was really impressed he wanted to be a doctor. Wow, I had never met someone who wanted to be a doctor. He was really intelligent; you could tell by his conversation and his vocabulary. Then we talked about his band, his favorite subject; he was the lead singer, and he played the guitar. He told me about the guys in his band. There was his brother Mark, who played bass; Steve Rudd, who played the drums; Rocky Lackey, who played the organ; Arvid Smith, who played lead guitar. Roger taught him how to play. I really enjoyed talking to him, but we could only talk a short time because his father was a long-distance truck driver, and when he called, he wanted to talk to them and he did not think phones should be used for anything but important things. He told me he would call the next day; I was thrilled. We talked every day. I had a regular babysitting job, so I stayed busy. He had things to do too, like washing his parents' cars and mowing the lawn.

He walked over to see me on Wednesday afternoon; we sat out on the front porch and talked and was interrupted by Evelyn, my little sister. But we worked around that. He also got to meet my mom, and of course, he already knew Ken. We enjoyed our time together; we never ran out of things to say; he always had a guitar pick in his hand, flipping it through his fingers. He showed it to me, and I told him I would keep it, but he said, "No." He had to have it to play his guitar. I melted every time he smiled at me. It was just getting dark when he got ready to go home, but before he went, he kissed me for the first time. I knew then that he was the right one for me. I was so in love. All I could do was think about him.

I talked to him on Thursday and Friday afternoon after I got home from babysitting all day. Even though I was babysitting in the neighborhood he lived in, I did not see him until Saturday night. There was no way I would let him come to the house where I was babysitting; it was just not done. Besides, he was busy practicing with his band, getting ready for gigs. He was so full of fun; we had so much to talk about. To me, he was breathtaking.

    He did not have a car and did not have a driver's license, so he walked to my house on Saturday night, so this was our first date. Because I was only fourteen, I would not have been able to go out anyway, so it did not bother us; we spent the evening in the den and listened to music. We both loved music; we danced and talked. He would kiss me when Evelyn was not peeking around the door, saying "Mmmm, I'm going to tell Mama."

Chapter 2

It was not long that school started, and I continued to babysit in the afternoons after school on Thursdays, Fridays, and Saturdays. He came over on Saturday nights. Sometimes, he had a gig on Fridays and was busy. I got up early on Saturday morning to curl my hair so I would be ready for my Saturday night date when I got home from work. We both liked to watch *Star Trek* on Friday nights, and if we were together, it was a understood we had to watch the show. He made arrangements for his band to play at the community center, a cinder block building with one door, which was a short ways from my house. Mark and I would let all our friends at school know they were having a dance. The cost was $1 per person. The building cost $5 to rent, and we provided drinks and snacks. Sometimes it was soda, Kool-Aid, or lemonade, cookies or chips—usually what we had at home. Nobody seemed to care; they just wanted to dance, listen to the music, or be with friends. It was such a happy time; we felt like we were on top of the world.

My cousin Nancy Haynes uses to come over and stay the weekend with me; she was dating Les Thompson, who was a friend of Roger's and Ken's. We always had fun together, the four of us; it was all about being in love and dancing and having parties, and whenever possible we would also have my cousin Wezi Haynes come too. She also liked a boy that lived down the street from our house. The three of us were like the Three Musketeers; I was the oldest, born in November 1951. Nancy Lynn was born in February 1952, and Wezi "Bonnie Louise" was born in April 1952. Back then, we walked all over the neighborhood without a care; we were always safe. We laughed played songs and talked about boys or our boyfriends and acted crazy. We could not help ourselves when we were together.

Saturday evenings were my favorite time because I knew I would have him all to myself for a few hours; he would come to my house, and it would be just us, except for Evelyn peeking around the door to see what we were doing. He would hold me and kiss me. That was when my world was perfect. I loved him so much, and I knew he loved me too.

His band, "The Avengers," got a gig on Sunday afternoons playing at the enlisted men's club on the navy base. That's when I did my homework. I knew I had to maintain my grades because if I did not, there would be no dates or dances. He did his homework on the bus ride home from school.

My birthday that year, 1966, was on Thanksgiving. I helped Mama cook dinner; we always had a huge crowd with all my siblings and friends. My oldest sister Bonnie always brought side dishes and extra desserts. Mom and I fixed the turkey, dressing, and gravy with vegetables and desserts too. Trust me, no one went hungry at our house ever. We talked on the phone that day, and he told me happy birthday, but Thanksgiving was a family holiday, and we each spent it with our families. He came to see me on Friday night with a senior class picture of himself for my birthday; he knew that was what I wanted. We were more and more in love. We cherished every minute we got to spend together. We would go out on the front porch for him to kiss me good night; sometimes it took thirty minutes, and as the weather grew colder, we were trying to keep each other warm. Things were getting pretty intense, but we were trying to behave.

December was a very eventful month for all of us with large families. There was my mom, Dorothy Bounds, my sister Bonnie, her husband, and two daughters. My four brothers were Will, Kline, Bob, and Ken, of which only two were married. Will and his wife Wanda and his son and two daughters and Kline and his wife Peggy. Roger's family was large too; there was his mom and dad; Jack Hilton; Sophie Hilton; his three brothers, Joe, Tommie, Mark; and his sister Jeannie. We were taught that this is what Christmas was all about, the birth of our SAVIOR JESUS CHRIST and our families; everything else came after that. His mom let him have a Christmas party at his house for the band and some of our friends. All the band members were there and quite a few friends. We had so much fun just sitting around, eating and talking. We never had time to do that kind of thing; if we were in the company of these friends, the band was always playing and we did not get to sit and talk. It was a great time, and we never left each other's side.

On Friday afternoon on Christmas Eve, his mother brought him to my house with this huge box that he could not wait for me to open. I started opening the box and what did I find was another box, just smaller. I opened that box, and there was another box, I went through this three more times until I came to a small thin box, about six inches long; finally, I could open my present. His mother and mine were really enjoying the whole thing. I opened the box, and it was a beautiful gold charm bracelet with a charm on it. The charm was the head of a guy with his name "Roger" engraved on it. What a wonderful gift it was. Like a wedding band, I never took it off. Then I retrieved his from under the Christmas tree. I watched closely as he opened it; when he had it open, he just smiled that wonderful smile of his and said "Thank you" and kissed me. I bought him a silver men's identification bracelet with his name engraved on the top "Roger" and my name "Betty" on the underside. His mother left and he stayed the evening until eleven o'clock. We spent most of the evening with my mom and Evelyn. Well, until we went outside to say good night. We enjoyed being together a few times while on Christmas vacation. I was still babysitting because it was Christmas vacation; it was all day not just after school and Saturdays.

We started back to school after Christmas, and he had a lot going on with school and the band; we were busy all the time. January brought another change to our relationship; we were intimate for the first time. With both of us being virgins, we thought we knew what we were doing, and we did not think about the risk we were taking. I was thrilled to hear his voice, his touch was wonderful, and he was all I thought about. I walked around in a daze, but I did my homework and continued to babysit. I saved my money because I knew we were going to the prom, and I had to buy a dress. February, the month of love and romance, everyone at my school was excited; we wanted to have a Valentines dance. Steve Rudd's mother was the secretary at our school, so Roger arranged for them to hold a Valentines dance at our school. What a frenzy, the girls were looking for dresses and the boys were looking for jackets or suits and ties.

I lucked out. I borrowed my sister-in-law Peggy's wedding dress; it was white and beautiful. Roger bought me red carnations to wear with it, and I bought him a white carnation to wear with his black suit. On the day of the dance, Friday the tenth, before Valentines, some of us girls at school got out early so we could bake heart-shaped red-velvet cakes with pink frosting at my house. For snacks at the dance, we also made punch. Then we went to the beauty shop and had our hair done. We could not stop talking about the dance this was our first school dance with long dresses because we were freshmen. We thought we were so grown-up. Mark had a date and was there, but so was Evelyn; she thought she should go too. She went, but the school got her back when the next dance came around for her grade, the officials at school would not let her go because she went to mine.

A lot of us had boyfriends that went to Berkeley High where Roger and Ken went to school. Our school was the new Goose Creek High, which was adding a grade each year, so we were the first freshmen, and our class would be the top class each year. We had a great time; we always did so much with so little. We appreciated everything we got to do. The dance was wonderful; we got to dance a few times because he was singing most of the time. We had fun anyway.

Now it was March, and we're getting ready for prom in April. I went shopping for my dress. I really took my time; I wanted it to be special. I finial decided on a pale yellow one. I knew it would look good with my red hair. I put it on layaway, and every week, I paid on it. Then I had to buy shoes and other things that girls need. Before we knew, it was time to go to prom; we were double-dating with Nancy and Les. Les went to get Nancy then Roger and then they came to my house. Roger bought me a beautiful orchid to wear with my dress, and I bought him a red carnation to wear with his white jacket because he had a red and yellow plaid bow tie and cummerbund. We thought we were hot stuff, and we were. The prom was wonderful we had dinner and then we got to dance all evening, which was a change for us, he is usually singing and sometimes I was his go-go dancer, but tonight he was all mine; it was dreamy. Nancy was staying at my house that night, and we talked about the prom most of the night. The next day was Saturday, and Roger was coming over to see me. I was so happy I could hardly wait for him to come over. When he was around, my heart pounded so hard, sometimes it was hard to breath.

Now prom was over with, and the end of school was just ahead; we were getting ready for Roger's and Ken's graduation. We all were studying for our end-of-the-year examination; our grades were so important. We all knew our grades would reflect on our choices after we finished school; we also were aware of our class placement.

Chapter 3

Monday, we were back in school, and I was back waiting to talk to him after band practice. While I was waiting, I did my usual chores: I washed clothes, cooked supper, and cleaned house; my mom was a stickler about her house, and I did not want to make her unhappy. She worked all day, so I did my part. After dinner, we would clean the kitchen and sweep the floor, ready for the morning. Sometime after dinner, Roger would call, and we talked for a for as long as we could get away with, and then I did my homework and prepared my clothes for the next day. Neat as a pin, that was how I rolled a preppy girl. Roger called that evening. I could tell he was upset about the rumor. Rocky had started saying I had cheated on Roger, he wanted to ask me about it so I hung up on him. I was so angry I would have hit him if he had been there. While I was waiting for him to call me back, I went to my mom's bedroom's doorway; we talked about school, her work (she went to work when my dad died the year before). We also talked about what I needed to do in the house the next day.

We heard a vehicle pull into the driveway with rocks flying. My mom sat up and said, "Who or what is that?"

I said, "That is hell on wheels. I hung up on Roger."

She laid back down while I went to answer the front door. When I opened the door, Les walked in and said, "I'm going to talk to your mom." As he said that, an arm reached in the door and pulled me outside and closed the door. All Roger could do was snarl. "Don't you ever hang up on me again," then he kissed me. I didn't get to talk for a while. When he finally let me talk, all I said was, "It is not true. I can't believe you could even think something like that, let alone ask me."

With the relationship we had as intimate as we were, I was beginning to build up a head of steam, and he saw it coming, so he kissed me again. When I calmed down, he apologized for even thinking I would do that. We continued making up until Les opened the door and said, "Betty, your mom said it is time for you to come in and for us to go, so say good night to Roger. I will start the car."

I kissed him one more time and said, "Good night and I love you and only you."

He responded with, "Good night and I love you too."

I went back into the house and told Mom good night and got ready for bed. Things ran smoothly after that hiccup.

We double-dated with Ken and his girlfriend, Tina. We went to the movies; we had a good time spending time with them.

I had to find a dress to wear to graduation. I went shopping, and with luck, I found two dresses. I bought them both. One had a white background with little light blue flowers with a shirtwaist with a full skirt that buttoned up the front. I was going to wear the blue Roger's favorite color; the other was yellow shirtwaist dress with an A-line skirt that buttoned up the front. I was finished with my school; after graduation, he would be finished too. I was hoping we could spend more time together. I anxiously waited for his call every evening. We had stars in our eyes when we were together, and like always, his wonderful smile made my heart pound. We were so in love we could hardly keep our hands off each other when other people were around. Nancy told us we were like gasoline and matches; we made a blaze.

We all got ready to go to the graduation; we were as excited as the seniors were. They were ready to be done with school. I sat with my mom; she was so proud of Ken because of the way he had worked to finish school. All she could do was beam and then cry as he walked across the platform. I, too, was proud of Ken; he was my closest brother and my friend too. Then it was Roger's turn to walk across the platform and get his diploma; you would have thought I was related to him as I clapped so loud. Most people knew who I was in relationship to him. After the ceremony was over, we waited for them to come back to us. Ken came to be hugged and kissed by Mom, then Tina and the rest of us that were there to congratulate him.

I waited with Nancy and Les we were double dating with them that night. After Roger went to see his parents and family members and told them goodbye, he came to find us; we were close by, and we had plans for the evening. We went to the beach to walk in the sand so we could relax. The tension of all the activities for graduation had worn us out, walking on the beach at night was our favorite time; we are both redheads, and the sun in Charleston, South Carolina, is not kind to us. We talked about what we were going to do through the summer and what kind of job Roger was going to get.

First, he had to get his license to drive. We were both looking forward to that. We had a nice evening. We were ready for summer but not a lot changed. I was continuing to babysit, and Roger got his driver's license and got a job driving a milk truck delivering milk to grocery stores. It was hot, hard work, lifting crates full of milk and milk products; he was glad to be working but always very tired. All of this bought another change to our relationship. We had Friday or Saturday nights for our dates, and now we went out alone unless Mark or Evelyn thought they should go with us. We did not want them around, but we took them anyway our parents just looked at us if we said no, so therefore, we relented.

One weekend, Nancy and Wezi came to stay the weekend with me. We had such a good time. Roger came to get us in his mother's convertible, the top was down, and we were going to the Target and Piggie Park Drive-ins. You go there to see who is there and to be seen; we got some sodas and talked to friends and waved to others. Then we decided to go back to Goose Creek. We were riding down the road. I was sitting in front as close to Roger as I could get. Nancy and Wezi were in the back. We had the radio playing and it was blaring so they could hear it too. Then the song "A Whiter Shade of Pale" came on, and we were singing it when Roger looked in the rearview mirror and gasped; both of those girls were sitting on top of the back seat waving at every car we passed, on Rivers Avenue just like parade queens. Roger told them they had better sit back in the seats before he got a ticket. It was so funny; we laughed all the way home. Those crazy girls could really have fun and did everything they could to aggravate Roger, but he had fun too; he was laughing as hard as we were. It was not our regular date, but we enjoyed them so much.

We went to the beach a couple of times with friends and had fun, but we were always careful so we would not get a sunburn. If Roger was not in the water, he always had his shirt on; we were not interested in getting a tan like everyone else. We never tanned; we just burnt to a crisp. But really, the beach in daylight was not our favorite place. That was what all the sun babies wanted to do, so we went sometimes not often. Don't get me wrong; we enjoyed being with everyone and being together. It was the heat and bad sunburns we had had before that made us leery of going.

Because we were working, our weeks flew by, and in June he had a birthday; he was now eighteen, a grown-up, or so we thought. He took me over to his brother Tommie's house, and I met Ida, his wife. She was beautiful with dark, shiny black hair. I will never forget what she said to Roger that day he had his arm around, and unfortunately, his hand was on my hip, not where it should have been, on my waist. Ida looked him straight in the eye and said, "Get your hand off of there, that does not belong to you."

July was more of the same; we did go to Charlotte, North Carolina, with his mother to see some of his relatives. I was wearing an olive-green tent dress with a high fold-over collar. I had just made it and wanted to show it to Roger and his mom, and it was also very cool to wear on a hot day. I love green; it's my favorite color. We walked around and sat in the car while his mother visited family. They were elderly as far as we were concerned, and we want to be elsewhere. We enjoyed spending the whole day together. We had never been able to do that before; we were just learning just because school was out, you could not spend your life together as the songs always said, but in real life, you have to work and be apart most of the day.

Roger was driving us home when a deer ran in front of us, and he hit it, even though he tried to miss it. We were on a long, dark road, and we had to walk to some people's house to find a phone. His mother reversed the charges and called his brother to come get us. I reversed the charges and called my mother so she would not worry because we were going to be late, like 2:00 a.m., getting home.

Chapter 4

We were really taking chances with our love life; it seemed we never saw each other as much as we wanted to, and we did not talk on the phone very long. Roger was always tired when he got home from work. And in order to talk to me, he had to go into the kitchen and sit on a barstool as they only had one phone. We had three or four phones in my house. I had one in my room and the kitchen had an eight-foot cord on it. I could move around or sit in the hall on the floor or go to my room. I had choices; he did not. I understood he was tired, so we did not talk long most evenings; we usually saw each other on Saturday nights because he was less tired after resting; when he was not washing cars and mowing the lawn for his mother, everything had to be done before his dad came home on the weekend. Because we did not talk and see each other as much, we took one risk too many: I got pregnant. I know we did not use protection. Where would we get it? Everyone in town knew us. He could not buy any; someone would have told his mother. It was inevitable: you play with fire, you get burnt.

Ken was planning a sweet sixteen birthday party for his girlfriend Tina on August 3, so we all pitched in to help. We all wanted it to be nice. Mom, Evelyn, Nancy, Jan (Nancy's sister), and I all got the house cleaned, fixed the snacks, and got the cake ready. We always enjoyed doing things like this; we all enjoyed being together. I was getting ready for the party and was in the bathroom putting on my makeup, which was very little; I did not like the feel of it on my skin.

I had other things on my mind. I told Roger and only him. I had looked up ways to make my period start. I also heard about things you could do at school. We were very worried and scared. I heard that you could take Quinine, and that would make you start, so I wrote it down on a piece of paper and put it in my purse so I could give it to Roger. He had to go and get it not me. Mama knocked on the bathroom door and asked me if she could enter. I opened the door, and she came in with that piece of paper in her hand. She told me she was looking for an ink pen to sign Tina's birthday card, and she found it in my purse. I didn't say anything; she asked me if I was pregnant. I told her, "I think so." It was not a pretty scene. My mother aged ten years right before my eyes. She told me we would talk later and left the bathroom. It's something I knew I would never forget.

I finished getting ready. I wanted to be right at the door when Roger arrived. I called him and told him she knew I was pregnant; that way, he was prepared. He came to the back door, something he had never done before. I was waiting for him when he came in and asked if I was all right. I told him yes, and that she was very upset; he said, "I knew that." We really did not know what to say to each other. He hugged me and kissed me and then someone called me to the other room. When I returned to the kitchen, he was gone. My mother, who was a lady to her fingertips, said to him, "You are an arrogant young man, and you need to leave."

He said, "Yes, ma'am," and left. I realized it was a setup that I was called to the other room. I was heart sick. I needed him to be with me and to reassure me that it was going to be okay, that we would get married as soon as possible.

That is not what happened, and what happened was awful. Mama had made plans to go camping with her brother, Uncle Hugh and Aunt Kitty, to Rocks Pond campground; she also insisted that I go, too, for a week. Oh my goodness, I was sick as a dog every morning. I would get up and start throwing up as I left the tent to walk forever to the bathroom. I learned quickly to have my toothbrush, toothpaste, and washcloth ready to go every morning. There was no slack given to me either; the only thing she did not make me do was go fishing. When Friday night came around, the campground hosted a dance for the teenagers at the community center. Mama made me get dressed and go. I went into the place and sat down. I was not dancing with anyone; after a while, I went outside sat and listened to the music, waiting till I could go back to the tent and go to sleep. The next day, there was another dance for everyone, I had to go again; this time, I did not bother to go in. I just sat outside. The next day, we were going home. I was so ready to be home, in my bed. I was so tired; I was exhausted. When we got home, Wanda my sister-in-law told me, "That's what happens when you are first pregnant."

I shortly learned that Roger was gone; his parents sent him to California to stay with his brother Joe who was in the navy. They sent him because they were in fear for his life; someone told them to watch out, that my brothers were looking for him. That was scary; I knew it was Bob and Kline. Kline just got out of the army. Bob was going to Vietnam, and Kline had been in Korea he was a paratrooper, and Bob was in the infantry. My brother Ken was going into the army, and Will was getting his family settled so he could go to Vietnam. They were a force to be reckoned with. I did not blame Roger's parents sending him to California.

That is not to say I was not angry that he was gone; I was—I was scared for him too. I was so angry with my brothers. I did not want to talk to any of them. How dare they think they should interfere in my life? It was no skin off their nose, and then I realized it was because of Mama.

I went to the doctor, and he confirmed all our fears. I was six weeks or so pregnant. But I already knew that you could not be sick every morning like I was and so tired and not be pregnant. I was miserable and everyone knew it. I lost my smile; I did not talk to anyone, but Trisha, my best friend that lived two houses down and across the street. She also was pregnant; she was a year older than me, and her boyfriend was in Vietnam.

My mother told me we were going to see an attorney. I was not happy about that I knew she was going to try and have Roger put in jail because I was underaged. I was not going to let that happen; he did not rape me. It was consensual; he had never pressured me in anyway. We went to see the attorney. When we went in, I only said hello and let Mama do the talking. She gave him all the information, and they talked as though I was not there; he told her he would have him picked up as soon as possible. When all was said and done, the attorney stood up and looked at me and told my mother he only needed me to confirm that Roger was the father of my child. I looked at my mother and then the attorney and replied, "I will give you six other names, but I will not give you his. You are not going to do this to him. He did not do this by himself. I was a willing partner." The attorney told Mama he was sorry; he could not help her if I would not cooperate. She did not speak to me all the way home. She was very angry, and I was going to have to live with that.

Will was painting the house down the street for Wanda and the children to live in so they would be close to us. Mama sent me down there to help; when I got there, Will and Wanda just looked at me like, "What are we supposed to do with you?"

I said, "Mama told me to come and help paint."

Wanda said, "You can't paint, you are pregnant."

Will replied, "Well, if she wants you to paint, you sit on the floor and paint baseboards and trim way down low. You will not get on the ladder."

School had started, and Mama was upset again because I could not go. She found and sent me another errand. I had to get up clean the house get dressed and walk to my sister Bonnie's house and help her watch the children she was babysitting. That was no easy feat; I was desperately tired, and I had to walk pass Roger's house to get there. When arrived, I was usually crying torn apart because he was gone. Bonnie would hug me and send me to bed to take a nap. I told her, "I have to go outside and watch the children."

She said, "You will not, you are too tired." She is thirteen years older than Evelyn and ten years older than me; she always treated Evelyn and me like we were her children, and I did not usually argue with her, but this time, I did. I told her Mama might call her to make sure I was helping.

She said, "I will tell her you are outside."

I replied, "What if she comes by at lunchtime, what then?"

She told me to go lie down she would handle it; I did. We talked all the time about things I did not know about, like the reason I was so tired. She explained I was in my first trimester and my body was getting used to me being pregnant, that my hormones were all over the place. I thank the LORD every day for Bonnie; she helped me get my head around what was going on. She prepared me for every step and change that was happening to me.

One day, Mama came home from work. Ken was with her; she was fixing her coffee she always had when she got home. She turned and told me, "She received a telephone call from her attorney, and he was relaying a message from Roger's attorney. Roger had told his attorney, that my baby was not his."

I came unglued. I screamed, "I do not believe it and you will not make me believe it no matter what you say."

"I know he did not say that, he wouldn't say that." I ran to the bathroom and locked the door. I was crying hysterically; that's when I reached for the razor blade. I was getting ready to cut my wrist when she and Ken started knocking at the door. I put the razor blade back in the cabinet because Ken asked Mama if he needed to break the door down. I told them no I was coming out. That was a dreadfully close call. I went to bed. I was not talking to anyone else. I quickly realized I could not take my own life like my father did two years before. If I died, my baby would die, and that was not an option.

Trisha was pregnant too. I was fifteen, and she was sixteen, in the evenings we were at each other's house, or we would walk down the street to see Wanda and the kids. I always love my nieces and nephew; they were precious children even when they were bad. Trisha started smoking while we walked and then I joined her. We smoked, drank hot tea and ate toast, played games, and had fun with Wanda. At around 11:00 p.m., we would walk back home; it made our evenings go by faster.

We did this until Trisha heard that her fiancé was coming home for Christmas to marry her. I was so happy for her; all her dreams were coming true. I was miserable. I wanted Roger to come home and marry me. It was very hard watching her prepare for her wedding, so I went to stay with Kline and Peggy in their apartment off Montague Avenue in North Charleston. I stayed with them for about six weeks. I was happy to be there. They both worked. Kline was on second shift at the papermill, and Peggy was a hairdresser. So would fix Kline lunch, and he would go to work. Later, Peggy would come home, and I would have dinner ready for us. She was fun and good company; she like to read magazines, and I read books all the time. I went home a couple of weeks before Christmas. Mama wanted me to come, so I went.

Our relationship was on the mend, and I wanted it to stay that way. I love my mama very much, and she knows I do. She needed time to get over the shock and being mad at me. I was happy to be home. I had been back for visits; it was not that far away, about ten miles, so it was not like I did not see Mama while I was living with Kline and Peggy. I did, but not for long periods.

We started getting ready for Christmas, putting up the tree, decorating the house outside, and planning presents; we always did this together. We shopped for Evelyn; she, after all, was the baby of our family. There were already five grandchildren in the family; we had fun planning and shopping for them. Mama had a unique way of shopping for all her children and their spouses. She would find out something that a couple needed together, like a small appliance or as an individual. For instance, if someone needed a toaster or an iron, they got that together or if they needed socks or sweatshirts, that's what everyone got. It made our shopping easier; we also had lunch out and enjoyed our days.

Around the twenty-second of December, Roger's mom called me and asked if I could come over to her house on Christmas Eve. Roger was going to telephone home, and he wanted to talk to me. She also told me she would come and pick me up. I told her, I would ask my mother and call her back. After I talked to Mama, she said, "Okay." I called Mrs. Hilton back and told her I would be able to come, and then I asked, "What time she would be coming to get me?" I can tell you I was in a state; I was going to talk to him and find out when he was coming home for us to get married. I was elated and everything was going to be fine.

Mrs. Hilton came to pick me up at the time she said. I did not worry about what was happening. It was going to be fine. I was going to hear his voice. I could hardly wait. We chatted going to her house about nothing important, just plans for Christmas and how everyone was. When we got to the house, I was nervous; walking into the house scared me stiff. As I went in the house, I was wondering who was there and what they would think about how I looked because I was almost six months pregnant and huge already. The shame you never expect springs up its ugly head. I knew Roger's dad would be there, and he was so nice; I just hesitated about going in. I went in because I wanted to talk to Roger. I convinced myself that was all that mattered.

Roger's dad smiled at me with concern in his eyes just like a grandfather would be looking at the mother of a new grandchild. Mark was on the phone talking to Roger, and I met Roger's oldest brother, Joe. Mrs. Hilton told me to go into the dining room and Mark would give me the phone so I could talk with Roger. Mark handed me the phone, and I noticed I was shaking. Don't ask me why, I have no idea. What I'd been hoping, crying and praying for was about to happen.

I said, "Hello," and the voice that I loved so much said, "Hi," just as he had always done. I could hear and feel my heart beating all over my body. I sat down on the stool they always kept by the phone.

Roger asked, "How are you?" And I told him I was fine but fat. He replied, "Not fat, just pregnant."

I said, "Yes, very. I love you."

He replied, "I love you too."

We continued to talk about everyday things for a while, and then I asked him, "When are you coming home?"

He replied, "I'm not sure yet."

I reminded him that I was due at the end of March, and things needed to be done before that.

He said, "I know but we need to talk about this."

I could not imagine what he was talking about; he was coming back to Goose Creek, and we would get married. I asked him, "What is there to talk about?"

He told me, "I've been wondering if that is what we need to do."

I was stunned and asked, "What do you mean 'if it's the right thing to do'? I'm almost six months pregnant. I can't undo that, and you told me we would get married."

He replied, "I know I did, but I'm wondering if that is what is best for us and the baby."

I could feel my body tighten up all over, and I could feel the tears well up in my eyes. My next emotion was, I got mad. How dare he say that to me. He left me holding the bag here; I was the one walking around with all the shame, looks of pity, and my mother so mad I could hardly stand it.

I went to the attorney and refused to tell him that he was the father to keep him out of jail, and now he was wondering if getting married was the right thing to do? I had to take some very deep breaths to hold on to my sanity. I wanted to explode. He asked, "Can we talk about this?"

I told him, "Go ahead, I'm listening."

He said, "I just think maybe we should do something different where the child is concerned."

In my mind, I was asking, *What are you saying? This baby is a living human being, and it is growing, and in a few months, it is coming.* Then I heard the words that I never expected to hear. "Maybe for the baby's sake, we should give it up for adoption?"

I know everyone in the house heard me gasp, even with the TV on. I was mad before, but now I was broken. I did not want to breath anymore I just wanted to die. My world crumbled. I said a very loud "No." Then he asked, "If you would, let me explain what I am thinking."

I wanted to hang the phone up, but I really did not want to. I wanted to keep talking to him and hear his voice no matter who was listening; the whole world could listen, I did not care. He continued to tell, "If we got married, we would have no place to live. I do not have a job, and we could not feed ourselves, much less a baby. So what else could we do?"

At that point, I did not know did not care I was not giving my baby away, and I preceded to tell him so. Mark came over to where I was and told me, "You cannot talk to him like that. It's Christmas eve."

Roger's brother Joe told Mark to be quiet, that I could say what I wanted to, I was fighting for my life and my baby. Roger then asked me to please think about what he said and that he would see me soon, and we would talk about it more then.

I replied, "Okay. I will think about it," but all I was going to do was get ready to get married when he came home. We said goodbye after he reminded me we were talking long distance and collect on his parents' phone. Hanging up that phone felt like I was cutting off my lifeline. After I put the phone on the cradle, I did not want to turn around, but I did there was nothing else for me to do. Mrs. Hilton was ready to take me home. All I said to the family was "Merry Christmas" and "Good night." The ride home was pretty much silent. I told her thank-you for bringing me home and Merry Christmas.

Chapter 5

Mama was waiting and I did not want to talk, but I did. I told her Roger was not sure when he would be home, but it would be before the baby is born. So we could get married. I did not tell her about him asking me to think about us giving the baby up for adoption not then. I can tell you I have never had a more miserable Christmas. My feelings about that phone call pretty much did me in. I would feel the baby kick, and I would think about who he or she would look like. Then I would think about giving he or she up and knowing I would never see the baby. That's how things were done. I was on an emotional roller coaster that was getting harder and harder to deal with. I did start to think about the baby first, and what it would be like to give my child to someone else and what that would mean to the child. I knew if we did not get married, I would almost certainly have to give it up, if only because of the ugly names it would be called. That was also breaking my heart.

I spent a lot of time by myself and cried myself to sleep every night. Tricia was almost ready to have her baby; she was so excited, and I was excited for her. All her world was coming together. She got married over the Christmas holidays; the Marines sent David home from Vietnam so they could get married. So she had a life of welcoming anticipation for her baby; she was buying baby clothes and supplies you need for a little one. Watching that was not easy; she was doing what I could not do. She had money from the baby's daddy and could go shopping I was not asking my mom for anything.

I went to the hospital with Tricia and her mom when she had her baby. It was a long night, so I went to look for coffee for Mrs. Kershaw and myself. I had not been to that hospital before so, I wondered around this hospital, so I got lost. Wandering around, looking for coffee, I got so lost and opened a door and found myself in the morgue. I moved so fast out of there; I don't know how I did not have my baby that night. Needless to say, I found someone to help me find the coffee. Tricia had a little girl. She was over the moon; that's just what she wanted. Later, Tricia's mom and I went back home. I cried myself to sleep again. Because I still did not know what to do, thinking about it made me very sad. When Tricia got home with her baby, I stopped spending a lot of time with her she was so busy with the baby, and all I wanted was for my baby to come so I could hold mine too.

Roger came home the first week of March; he called me and asked if I would meet him at the courthouse downtown Charleston on Friday afternoon so we could apply for the marriage license. Mama and Ken took me down there because Roger told me he had to pick up his dad from work when we were through. I did not think much about that because my mother had to be there because I was underage and could not apply for a license without her consent.

We met at the outside door of the courthouse; he had Mark with him, and I had Mama and Ken. He said, "Are you ready?" I said yes and in we went; he did not touch me or hardly looked at me. I was patient; this was hard for him too. After we filled out the paperwork, we went back outside. He thanked my mother for coming and turned to me and said, "I must go and get my dad from work." He never even touched me, much less kiss me. I was heartbroken all over again. I had not seen him for seven months and only talked to him once or twice in all that time. Was I expecting too much? I did not think so. It felt like he was saying "I ran by here on the way to pick up my dad." I felt in my heart he was being orchestrated by someone else; you know, the last time he kissed me was the night my mom found out I was pregnant. That was a long time. I just wanted him to touch me, kiss me, so I could feel like I was important to him. He never did, and I felt so alone and abandoned.

After Mama, Ken, and I got back in the car, I could not talk to them. I just sat there while we rode home, but on the way home, we had a flat tire. Ken told us to stay in the car, and he would take care of it, so we did. While we were waiting, Mama said to me, "If you don't get married, and give the baby up for adoption, I will send you to Kansas to stay with Wanda and the children for the summer." By then, I had told her that Roger and I were talking about doing that and I had not made up my mind. I think she saw how vulnerable I was and was trying to help me make that decision. Sometimes, your parents know you better than you think. She was trying to make me understand there would be a life for me after the baby was born. I did not think so. I thought I would die without my baby and Roger; what was there to live for if I give them up? All I could reply was "I don't know."

That was when I realized that no matter what you think about, the LORD always has the last word in your decisions; He always finds a way to help you when you belong to him. Very quietly in my mind, I was reminded that Roger and I were of two very different religions and that it would cause trouble when it came to how our child was brought up. He was Catholic, and I was a Seventh-Day Adventist. These two religions are very, very different, and I knew I could not become a Catholic or raise my child as one. This is what the Bible means when it tells you not to be unevenly yoked. Sometimes it's the things you don't want to talk about or think about that help you understand why you must do something, completely different than what you planned to do. I pushed it to the back of my mind. I did not want to think about it. I planned to get married, and that's what I was working toward.

I went shopping on Saturday to buy a dress to get married in; it was bright yellow like daffodils, my favorite color. Just looking at it made me happy. In my mind, I planned how I was going to wear my hair, makeup, shoes, all the trimmings. Finally, Tuesday came—the day I was getting married. I was going to see Roger and we would be so happy. He would tell me he was still in love with me, and we would be together for the rest of our lives. No more worries, just us and the baby that I wanted to name Richard Matthew. *Richard* after his brother and mine; we both had brothers named Richard. *Matthew* after Roger; that's his middle name. We would call him Dicky; everything was going to be fine.

Mama was still home; she was waiting for me to go before she went to work. As I was getting ready, I heard the front do open, and then I heard Kline and Bob talking to Mama. I was mad and terrified at the same time. I knew they were the ones that had been looking for Roger before he went to California, and they were not going to cause trouble today of all days, not on my wedding day. I called Mama from my room and told her I had called Roger and told him to meet me at Tricia's house. Then I finished getting dressed and called bye to Mama as I went out of the door. I did not see my brothers, nor did I want to, not that day.

I got to Tricia's house before Roger did. She was busy with the baby; however, she and her mom told me how nice I looked in my new dress. I felt very confident. I chose not to look in the mirror a lot because all you could see was my big baby bump. I felt like that's all you saw when you looked at me. I was hoping that was not all Roger saw. I wanted him to see me as the girl he was going to marry. Roger finally got there, and yes, Mark was with him. I did not anticipate that. I guess I should have after Friday. I got extremely uncomfortable when I saw Mark. This is now how I pictured my wedding day. I wanted to be alone with Roger, so I could tell him how much I loved him. I also wanted him to reassure me that we were doing the right thing.

The whole situation made me very angry and upset. I know it was not Mark's choice to be there; this was Roger's mother's doing. Just like the call from the attorney's office, when he asked me if I wanted to give the baby up for adoption, to which I answered no. After we got in the car and Roger started driving, then came the next bombshell; he had to go by his mother's attorney's office to drop off some papers that pertained to her custody battle for his nephew, Peter. This was to frighten me, and it did. I think I knew what his mother was doing before we ever got there. I knew he was going to ask me to go in with him, and when he did just that, I felt a great sinking in my heart.

This was the follow-up to the questions before about us giving the baby up. We went in, and he went to the receptionist and handed her the papers and told her who he was and what the papers were. She replied, "Please wait a minute, Mr. Lawrence wants to talk with you both." He turned and looked at me and said okay. Now I was sure I was right about the whole thing. I could feel the rage and the hurt building in my heart and soul. I wanted to say, "No, I'm not talking to anyone" and then run. But I was not raised that way. I knew I was going to have to deal with this head on. My heart was beating so fast I could feel it pounding in my chest. She did not give us time to even sit down to wait; she ushered us right in to Mr. Lawrence's office. It was a setup, the whole thing, from bringing the papers here and him wanting to talk to us. For some reason, I did not blame Roger. I just knew his mother did this to us. I would not let myself remember that Roger had already asked me if I thought we should give the baby up. I just wanted to believe in my heart that he understood how I felt after I told him NO at Christmas. He told me he was coming home to marry me, and he did. Why get the license? Why get dressed up to get married and then come here to do this? Did they think I would change my mind, or was this a lesson in how to not trust anyone? I was doing everything I could to not cry or scream, "I'm not doing this." But again, I was not raised that way. I had to present myself as a lady always. We all sat down in the office with me in one chair and Roger well away from me in another; he was not near enough to even hold my hand. I felt isolated, by myself; he really had not touched me all morning, I realized—that should have told me something. Mr. Lawrence told us thank you for coming to see him; he glanced at Roger and then he locked his eyes on mine and preceded to ask me if I had thought about our telephone conversation.

Because I did not answer him, he turned to Roger and asked him the same question. I waited for Roger to answer him and tell him we were on our way to get married just like he promised me at Christmas. Roger never said a word; he just stared at me. So now I knew the decision was all mine. How unfair was that? Not what I expected, that's for sure. I want to scream and say NO, but I did not. I looked at Roger and said, "Okay, I am not marrying you and we will give the baby up for adoption."

Mr. Lawrence smiled and said, "That's fine, here is my card. Please have someone call me when the baby is born."

Roger shook hands with Mr. Lawrence, and we went to the car. Roger asked me if I wanted to go with him to pick up the marriage license. I told him yes, I did. We were on our way to downtown Charleston. I did not want him out of my sight. I thought he would say, "No, let's get married." How could my mind work like that? Well, I was sixteen years old and so in love. I thought the sun and moon would not shine without him. I was holding on to hope that this day would not end like this. I wanted him to hold me, kiss me, and tell me he loved me. In my mind, a whole different scenario was taking place.

While we were on our way to town, the car he was driving broke down. Roger got out of the car with Mark to see what was wrong. Apparently, the fan belt had broken so Roger leaves me in the car with Mark while he goes to get a fan belt. He came back and repaired the car. When he finished fixing the car and got back into the vehicle, he said, "We are going back to Goose Creek." He was taking me back home without getting the license and without getting married. I was devastated, but I still did not give up. I told him I wanted to go to his house first. I thought if I could just talk to him alone. We could figure this out. When we got to his house, we walked in and he asked me if I wanted something to drink and I replied, "No, thank you." I then sat down on the sofa, and lo and behold, Mark sat down in the chair across from me and Roger went to the kitchen. I really saw that no matter what I did, he was not going to be alone with me at the house.

Therefore, I asked him to take me home. I figured Mark was not needed for that. I was wrong. He got up and went out to the car with us. He drove up to the sidewalk at my house, and I got out of the car. That was the first time he did not walk me to my door or say anything; he just drove off. I wanted to die. What a wedding day; the shame I felt that he did not want me or the baby, just about took my breath away. I held it together until I got into the house, and then the tears came. Thank goodness, no one was at home. I collapsed on my bed and cried like the world was at an end and my life was over. The things I thought as I cried were horrible; I really wanted to end my life. I knew I could not do that; the child in my body did not deserve that. I had to take care of it even if no one else wanted it. I knew I said okay to the adoption, but how was I going to do that? I really didn't think I could; I did not think I was strong enough to walk away from this child I loved so much. I continued to cry until I went to sleep. I woke up later when Evelyn came home from school. I did not get up or open my door when she knocked. After a while, I heard her call Mama, and shortly thereafter, Mama came home.

When she knocked, I answered her and told her I was all right, just tired and was sleeping. She left me alone after that because she knew I had not gotten married. I just did not want to see anybody yet. After dinner, she came to my door and told me I needed to eat so I got up and went to the bathroom and put a wet cloth on my eyes so the swelling would go down; then and only then did I go to the kitchen. I was not hungry, but I ate something to keep Mama happy.

I stayed home until it was time for the baby to be born. I did not go anywhere so anyone would see me. I was like a zombie. Thankfully, I only had to wait twenty-two days before the baby came.

After, I went into what I thought was labor around 5:00 a.m. on April 3, 1968. I woke my mom and told her I thought the baby was coming. She timed my contractions and then she called the doctor. We got ready to go to the hospital. Mom and my brother Bob took me downtown Charleston to Roper Hospital; that's where Dr. Finger told her to bring me. As we were checking in, someone asked my brother, "Is this your first baby?" And he replied, "Yes, it is."

He will never understand how much I appreciated that. We got there, and we had plenty of time; it was going to be a long, arduous day. I went from being uncomfortable to being in agony. My mother stayed with me most of the time when they would let her. She kept me from pulling my hair out. I would grab the bars on the bed and then my hair and start to pull because I hurt so bad. She would take my hand and uncurl my fingers to get the hair out of them. She did this over and over; one time, I was on the verge of screaming and she said, "Scream if you want to," and I said, "I will not scream." I did not scream even though I wanted too. About 5:15 p.m., I dilated enough to go to the delivery room, and that is all I remember; they knocked me out.

I woke up long enough to understand it was all over, and the pain was pretty much gone, but so was my baby. I was so full of panic, I was not allowed to get up and I was in a private room. After everyone left, I called Roger and told him I had given birth to our baby. He told me he would see me tomorrow. I told him to call first. I did not know who was coming to the hospital. I was scared for him; if my brothers came, it would not be pretty.

The next morning, my mom called to check on me and said I would have visitors later. *What did that mean?* I wondered. So later in the day, Roger called and told me he was in the parking lot of the hospital on a pay phone. I told him not to come up because he might be seen by someone coming to see me. We did not talk long even though I wanted to. He asked me if I had seen the baby, and I told him no they would not let me see it or tell me if it was a boy or girl because I was giving it up for adoption. I answered his questions about how I felt and if I was okay. He called me again the next day, and I told him the lawyer had been to see me and asked me if I would be ready to sign the final papers the next day. I told him I would. I stayed in the room and only ventured out one time with my cousin Karen and her friend.

The next day, a young nurse dropped off a paper for me to fill out to fill out before I was released; it was the birth certificate for the baby. It was supposed to say "Bonds Baby." What it said was "Bonds Baby Boy." When I read that, I just stared at the words with growing horror. I had a SON. Dicky was here. I wanted to see him, hold him; I started crying. The more I cried, the more upset I got. My room was next to the nurses' station, and they heard me and came to see what was wrong. I handed a nurse the paper, and she turned white. They finally got a hold of Dr. Finger on the telephone; he was in the hospital. I knew the minute he got to the nurses' station. Everyone could hear him; he was cussing a blue streak. He demanded some medicine and came to my room and gave me a shot to knock me out. I woke later in the night very out of it. Thank goodness there were no evening visitors; well, I guess there were no visitors. I was asleep. I walked down to the nursery to see if I could see my baby, but they told me no because I had agreed to give him up for adoption; they kept him in the back with the nurses.

The next morning came, and I was still groggy and really nervous. I kept thinking about the baby. I did not want to leave him there. I wanted to take him home with me; I had given my word to Roger and the attorney. I felt like I just wanted to shut down. I would have liked another shot so I could just sleep and not wake up. Thinking about it was driving me crazy. Gently, God reminded me I had to do what was best for my son. I was not married; he did not have a father. How was I going to take care of a baby? When Mr. Lawrence and his secretary came, he asked me if I was ready to sign the final papers. I told him I was ready. I was shaking as I signed the papers, and my heart felt like it was jumping out of my chest. The tears just rolled down my face. I did not try to stop them or even wipe them away, and I stayed silent until they left because I knew I would change my mind and tear the papers to shreds just like my heart was shredding. I knew deep inside of me, I would never ever be the same person I was before I signed those papers.

It's hard to explain how devastated I was, I was so hurt, I felt broken inside, but at the same time, I knew I would always love Roger and our son; it was a part of me I had to live with. I knew I would mourn for them as long as I lived. I cried more tears over them than I thought possible. Sometimes I wanted to hate Roger, but I knew I never would, and as far as the baby was concerned, I would mourn for him every day of my life and look for him every time I saw a little redheaded boy. My mom and I cried all the way home from the hospital.

Chapter 6

When I came home, I stayed close to home again. I was waiting for my six-week checkup, so I could leave and go to Kansas. I just wanted to be away from everyone here. I was also missing Wanda and Will's children. I felt like they were part of me too. I had changed diapers, fed, dressed, and generally took care of them when I got a chance. I needed to love them and hold them. I went out there the week after my checkup, the third week in May 1968. Wanda had come to live with us after she married Will, and he had to stay in Germany for a while; we were very close. Being with Wanda was always fun; we laughed about the craziest things. We did not care we enjoyed each other's company. She married Will when she was the age I am now. She understood me, and I was able to talk to her. She did not think I was crazy for doing what I did, and when I said I still loved Roger and the baby, she understood.

I got sick while I was in Kansas. I had to stay in bed for three days. I felt like someone was stabbing me in the stomach, and I was throwing up. We knew it was not my appendix because I did not have a fever. I just road the pain and sickness out till it got better. It really scared me. I thought I was going to die. When something like that takes place, you wonder where your life is going and where you will end up. We got a coupon to have pictures made so I made Wanda and Beth new matching dresses; she did not have a photo of the two of them like she had with Bobby and Christine. I also made a new dress for myself and had a picture made. I was going to send it to Roger, so he would know a was back to my old self, but without a heart because mine was dead.

I stayed in Kansas for six weeks. I enjoyed my time there meeting some very interesting people. We only left the small town of

Dennison when someone would come and take us to the town of Holton. We walked to the dairy to buy milk, we walked to the post office, we walked to the store to buy groceries, and we walked to a lady's house on Main Street who had a telephone switchboard in her living room to make a long-distance telephone call; it was like living in a bygone era.

I met a man at the one diner in town; before we finished the conversation, I knew everything about him—that he lived there, and he was a crop duster. He offered to take me flying; believe me, that was not on I had been in a small plane once before going from Lincoln, Nebraska, to Omaha, Nebraska, to catch a big plane to Charleston, South Carolina. I was not getting on a small plane, you could see the ground through the holes in the floor again. He asked me out. I told him no, that I did not think that was a good idea that, I was only visiting for a while. Then he told me he was serious that he wanted to marry me. I very politely declined. Yikes, that was very strange. I was ready to go home then.

I was flying home, thinking about the strange things that had happened to me while I was pregnant and afterward. I had three different men say they wanted to marry me and none of them were the man I wanted to marry. One was a captain in the army that came home with my brother early in my pregnancy, and one I'll never reveal because he was drinking and married, duh, and the guy in Kansas. It made me think why they said those things and why Roger did not want me. I knew I was in deep trouble in my heart and mind. Roger was gone, the baby was gone, and I had to leave it behind me; but how do you do that?

When I got off the plane, I was glad to see my mama waiting for me, and she was glad I was home. Even through all the hurt and pain we went through during and after my pregnancy, we were close. I know she was hurt but more than that, she was mad, and it took her a while to get over being mad, she also blamed herself as a mother.

After being home a day or two, I went to see Patricia and her little girl across the street; she was in the backyard hanging out diapers. She was busy so stooped down to look at the baby; she was beautiful, just like her mother. I was tickling her feet when Trisha came over to us; we were talking for a while. I told her about my trip and staying with Wanda. She had been close to Wanda too; we used to walk down our street to go to Wanda's just about every night while we were pregnant. We played cards, and I helped Wanda with the children getting them ready for bed. Then we would play cards, drink hot tea, and eat buttered toast. We always enjoyed our time doing that. While we were talking, she asked me what I was going to do now. I told her I was going to try and go back to school. She asked if they were going to let me, meaning, the school officials. I told her I was going to ask, that was all I could do. She looked me straight in the eye and said, "It will be like you never had a baby. What if GOD does not let you have any more children because you gave yours away?"

I was dumbfounded with horror. I took a deep breath to cover my hurt and said, "I pray that won't be the case."

I knew she was somehow feeling it was not fair that I was going back to school, and she was hanging out diapers. I thought a lot about what she said, knowing her husband was in Vietnam and she had not seen him since they got married. What I would have given to be in her shoes, to have Roger and my baby back, she had no idea. I was real hurt that she asked me that; she just added another worry to my life, and it was a real worry for me, so I did not see her very much after that.

Life continued. I had to think about going back to school, getting clothes and things ready for that. I like to sew, so I was busy making clothes to wear. Some of my friends from school came by to see how I was and invited me to a dance that was being held at the gymnasium on the base. I told them I would think about it. I was not sure that was something I could do. Roger's band (The Avengers) almost always played at the dances I used to go to, and I was very afraid of the memories.

Just like the last time, I went to a dance my mom told me I should go, that I might enjoy it and my friends. I wanted to tell her I did not have anything in common with them anymore, but I did not want to upset her, so I went. I danced a few times and that was okay, but I could see the questions in the eyes of my friends. I know they wanted to know what happened to me and Roger and my baby. I let them know that Roger and I decided to give the baby up for adoption. We knew we could not take care of ourselves, much less a baby; that we felt we were doing the right thing for the baby. It was us that had to suffer the consequences of what we had done.

Chapter 7

I continued going to the dances with my friends, met new friends and connected with people I had gone to school with, but never really got to know. A friend's mother asked me if I was dating, and I told her I had been to the movies with some old friends, but that was all. She said she had a coworker that wanted to ask me out. Since she was my friend's mother, I said I would meet him and talk to him and then decide. She arranged for us to meet, and I told him I would go out with him. He was a sailor working part-time with her. I got ready to go out with him. I had no misgivings or worries about it. He came and picked me up and met my mother. She told us not to be late. I answered, "Yes, ma'am."

He was very nice; he walked me to his car and opened the door for me to get in. We talked about where he was from and his family, his car, and the navy. It was not dark; it stayed daylight later in the summer, and because we were going to a drive-in movie, we went to the Target Drive-In on Rivers Avenue, the local hangout. We ordered sodas and continued to talk, and then out of the blue, he asked me what I thought about premarital sex. I took a drink of my soda and told him that I thought it was wrong, really wrong. He smirked at me and said, "That's not what I heard."

I told him, "I am sure you heard just that and because you know my history, you thought I would be a good time. Well, I will tell you now more than ever, before, I believe it is wrong. I also think you should take me home now." He started to hem and haw about it, so I told him, "Look, if you don't want to take me home, I will call one of my brothers to come and get me. See those dimes in my Weejuns, I never leave home without them, so I always have money to call for help, and with four big brothers, all I need to do is call."

He replied, "Okay, okay, I will take you home." He drove like a maniac and cursed like a sailor; when I got out of the car, I told him to lose my phone number and never speak to me or about me again. I was not happy to say the least; whether my friend's mother was thinking I needed a date or trying to help, what she told him was not something I wanted people to be told especially someone I might date. People wag their tongues about things better left unsaid. I learned I did not want anyone else to fix me up with a date.

After inquiring, it was decided I could go back to school; it was very strange to go back. I felt a hundred years older than the people that were there, even some of the teachers that had never been married or given birth. I did go to the doctor and get an excuse not to take physical education. I was not undressing in from of those girls with my stretch marks. Being a redhead and having strawberries and cream skin added to having a baby that weighed nine pounds, four and three-quarter ounces, my skin was still in bad shape and probably always would be—nope, not doing that. I was a good student never failed anything, but I never studied that hard either. I liked going to school. I had a very inquiring mind and wanted to learn things. I also read all the time I liked gothic, romance, and regular fiction, but mostly love stories that ended with a happy ending. I was not alone; some of the teachers liked them too. In fact, we would swap books when we finished with them.

Just before school began, I started dating a sweet guy named Doug; we had been to school together before, but I never got to know him. We got acquainted at the dances I had been going to. I enjoyed his company; he was a nice, well-mannered, and a fabulous dancer; and he loved to dance like I did. During the week, Monday through Thursday, we saw each other at school and talked on the phone in the evenings. He came to see me on either Friday or Saturday and night sometimes both. We listened to music, danced, and talked about school and what was going on there. Sometimes, my mother would take us to a dance and pick us up because he did not have a car, and when he came to see me, I was usually at Wanda's house babysitting. She was working at the Kreme King, which was a sandwich shop and ice cream parlor combined. She went to work after I got home from school. I did laundry, cleaned house, and prepared dinner for the children. Then it was bath time and bedtime, drinks of water, then I have to potty. I will never forget those times with those children; they had me in the palms of their hands. I just did not let them know it; they filled a big whole in my heart.

I was out of school one day, sick, when I was told by a friend of mine later that our teacher said they would have a good class today because I was. Betty was absent and would not be there to ask questions. I asked my teacher why she said that, even though I knew what her answer was going to be, and I quote, "When you are in class, you ask a lot of questions, and I don't have all the answers." I started laughing and she asked me why I was laughing. I had to admit that I had heard that before. My mother got so aggravated with me one time because I was asking questions about the Bible. She told me I would have to wait until I got to heaven and ask GOD because she did not have the answers and GOD did.

At Christmas, Doug bought me a promise ring. I was so surprised, but I accepted it and told him I was his. We continued to date; we did not go out a lot other than dances, having fun where we found it. I went to the prom with him. We doubled with one of his friends and had a marvelous time. He got his driver's license, and my mom let him drive her car if we wanted to go out for a while. We stayed close to home; he did not have a job. He drove me and my cohorts around to get companies to buy advertisements for our yearbook. I was the business manager, which was part of my job. Then he got a job driving a school bus; the juniors drove the buses. He was also in chorus club and drove them to the concerts.

On March the 22, 1969, Doug went with me to Ken and Tina's wedding. Ken was in the army and Tina had until June to graduate. After they were married, she came to live at our house while she finished school. She and Evelyn were together most of the time. I had things to do, like clean house, cook dinner, and babysit after school. I did not spend a lot of time with them.

Doug told me he had a job that was going to start as soon as school was out; he would be driving a drycleaner's truck, picking up and delivering peoples laundry and clothes that had been cleaned.

He was really counting on us getting married after we graduated the next year; we would be seniors together. We would finish in the first graduating class of Goose Creek High School, 1970.

I knew I could not marry him. I was far too old for him emotionally. I talked to my mother about it, and she told me I should break it off now instead of later; it was not fair to him. I told him I was giving him his ring back, that I could not marry him the next year; he asked me to keep it and to continue to date him till the next year, but I knew I could not do that because just thinking about being free was very liberating. I knew it was not wise to let it linger; I told him he was wonderful, fabulous guy, sweet and caring, and he would have no trouble finding someone else. It was very hard to do, but I knew it was the right thing to do. School was almost over for the year, and he would not have to see me and that would help.

I had to go to summer school to take eleventh-grade English and a math class so I would be in the senior class the next year. I was going to graduate with my class, even though I had missed a whole year of school. It was not a problem for me. I always carried more classes than I needed, so picking up a couple of classes was not hard. I made good grades; I listened in class and did my homework. I never could understand how someone could come to school without their homework. I would have been too embarrassed to call attention to myself for not having it. I liked to read, so I always read the required chapters so I would have some knowledge of what the teacher was talking about. I also like talking to my mom about what I was studying.

I started summer school and was busy with keeping house and cooking dinner and doing my homework. I rode with a friend back and forth to school; she was a year behind me but was getting some extra credits, and some of the classes were easier in summer school. I think I had about three weeks to go when Mama needed to go to the bank. I had her car, so I went at lunchtime, which was after school to take her. We went into the bank, and when we came out, the car would not start; my mom worked for my uncle at an auto parts store, so she told me to go back into the bank and call the store and ask my cousin to come see what was wrong. He came right away and got the car started, but he did not come alone. He had a friend with him, someone my mother knew very well.

His name was Carl Barrs. He was beautiful, handsome, and had impeccable manners. He spoke first to my mom telling her he had been at the store and came with my cousin Kenny to help. They were able to sort it out immediately. She thanked them, and off they went. I took her back to work, and as we were driving, she said, "You have not been out lately."

I said, "No, but that's okay."

She then told me Carl was a very nice young man, and I should maybe date him. I told her I did not want to date Carl. I knew who he was, and he surely did not want to date me. I left it at that, done and over.

A few days later, I got a phone call from a friend named Terry. He told me Carl wanted to go out with me, and he wanted to arrange it and he wanted to go out with my cousin Nancy. I told him I did not know if that could be arranged. I needed to think about it, and I had to ask Nancy what she thought. I called Nancy, and we decided, "Okay, we would go." I knew Terry and his whole family. I used to go to his house, and we all hung out together. I did not know he knew Carl; Terry told me he and Carl had gone to school together and were friends, small world. Nancy came to stay with me for the night, and guess what, Carl and Terry never showed up. So since we were dressed and ready to go out, out we went. We went to a bar and drank Tom Collins and danced with some sailors we met. They decided to buy us a real drink, and we drank it, and one more, but we were not stupid. We went to the restroom together and decided we needed to go home. We went back and told them the dancing was lots of fun, but we had to go. I had to work the next day. We gathered our things and out the door we went. We laughed all the way home because we knew we had let our guard down, and we could have been in trouble if they had given us a hard time. When we got back to my house, we told Mama good night and went to bed. There we were lying there in the bed, laughing and giggling. She told me the room was spinning to the left, and I told her, nope, it was going to the right. Trust me, I never did that again; that was a learning curve for me.

Chapter 8

We had a lot of parties and dances because all of us liked to dance. So we decided to have a party at Kline and Peggy's house. They had a beautiful house and a great patio for dancing. We called everyone and planned snacks, sodas, and plenty of music. Tuesday that week, I got a call in the middle of the week. It was Carl Barrs.

I said, "Hello, how are you?"

And he replied, "I am calling you to apologize for last weekend."

I replied, "Oh, last weekend? Why is that?"

He said, "I really did not stand you up. Terry made the arrangements with everyone but me. He never told me I had a date with you."

"I see. Can he corroborate that?" I asked.

He said, "He can, or I will break his neck." Then he laughed.

I asked him, "Is there anything else you would like to say to me?"

"Yes," he replied, "will you go out with me Saturday night?"

I asked him, "Why not Friday night?"

He told me, "I work on Friday nights. I work at AVCO Lycoming. I work the second shift. That's why I was with Kenny when we came to fix your mother's car."

"Oh, you were working last Friday, the night of our date?"

"Yes, I was!" he said.

I told him we were having a party at Kline and Peggy's house on Saturday, that he was welcome to come.

He asked me, "What time?"

I told him 7:30 or 8:00 p.m. He replied, "I will be there."

I said, "Fine, I will see you there."

Before I could say goodbye, he asked me if he could ask me one more question. "What do you do in the mornings?"

I told him, "I am in summer school, taking some extra classes."

Then he asked me, "What time do you get out of class?"

"Usually around 11:30 a.m.," I replied.

I heard a buzzer in the background and wondered what it was; he said, "That's the buzzer. I have to go back to work. Can I call you tomorrow?"

I told him, "That's fine."

He said "Bye" and was gone.

Nancy called and said she wanted to bring a girlfriend from work to the party with her. I told her that was fine; her name was Cara Murrillo. I told her Carl called and said he was coming. Her answer was, "Wow, when did this happen?" I told her he called to apologize because of last week, that Terry had not told him he was arranging the date, and he was working on Friday night. I told her he asked me for a date on Saturday, so I told, him we were having a party Saturday night. Therefore, I asked him to come to the party, and he said he would be there, so we will see if he comes. Oh, and he said he would call me tomorrow afternoon before he goes to work."

She said, "I will see you Saturday, bye."

Carl called me the next day after I got home from school. We talked a while. I told him I knew of his brothers and his sister was, that I had met his older brothers because they were friends of my brothers. He informed me that he knew my brothers, especially Ken, that he drove Ken's bus route when Ken graduated from high school at Berkeley. We talked a while, then he had to eat and get ready for work. I told him, "Bye," and he told me, "I will call you tomorrow, bye."

The next day, he called again; he wanted to know if it was okay if he brought Terry and Dave Lee with him to the party. After I thought about it, I said, "Sure." That way, Nancy and Cara will have someone to dance with. I called Nancy and told her what I had said to him, and she said that was fine with her. I just did not want them to be surprised the night of the party. Carl called me every day when I got home from summer school. I was getting excited to finally meet him face-to-face so we could talk and get to know each other. He was a lot of fun to talk to, and he loved his car. He had a 1967 pea-green mustang, and he told me all about it.

Saturday finally arrived, and I got ready to go to the party. Mama took me over there; she was going to stay a while; the house was full of her children and some of her nephews. We did not leave anyone out when we had a party—family or friends. Carl strolled in with Terry and Dave. We introduced everyone and started dancing. We laughed and sang with the music; we were getting down. I wish we had taken movies of my brothers dancing; they could boogie. I danced with them too. Carl had just sat down next to Kline, and they were talking about cars. I was standing in front of them when Carl said, "Do you want this chair?"

I told him, "No, I was fine." Kline looked at me and said, "Sit on Carl's knee."

I just about fell over; that was so not like my brother. When I paused as to think about it, he said, "Go on, he is almost like family."

Carl patted His knee and said, "It's okay, I won't break, I promise." Like I thought he would he was five feet eleven; he wore a large shirt. He had big shoulders and beautiful legs. I saw him in cutoffs the day he came with Kenny to fix the car at the bank for Mama. I turned and sat on his knee; he said, "See, I did not break," laughing with Kline. That's when I looked at the patio doors. Doug was standing in the kitchen, watching me. What was he doing here? I did not know he was coming. After he left the door, I told Kline and Carl I was going to get a Pepsi, and I asked if I could get them something; they said no, they were fine.

I went into the house to see what was going on. Mama was sitting in the den in the recliner, and Doug was sitting in a chair. I said hello and asked Mama if she wanted something to drink, and she also told me she was fine, so I looked at Doug. He had a Pepsi in his hand, so I nodded my head and turned and went back into the kitchen. Evelyn was standing in the kitchen. When she saw me, she turned and walked out; that's when Doug spoke my name behind me. He looked down at me and said, "She did not know you had a date tonight and she asked me to come to the party." I could have wrung her neck; she had no business interfering in my life. I told Doug that we were having a party and a lot of friends and family had been invited, that I had never dated Carl'; this was the first time I had met him after he came with Kenny to fix my mom's car.

I went back outside and did not come back in until later. We all continued to dance, and every now and then, I felt eyes on my back, but I just ignored it.

Nancy and Cara came over to where Carl and I were talking; she had Terry and Dave in tow to tell me she needed to take her friend home. Terry said to Carl, "Let's all go."

Carl told him, "That would be great."

I said, "Hold on. I've got to ask Mama about this, just wait a minute." I turned to go into the house, and they all came with me. Carl walked by the counter in the kitchen and picked up his six pack of beer, put it underneath his arm and followed me into the den. Then he proceeded to tell my mom that we were going to take Nancy's friend home to West Ashley, that it would be safer if the guys went with the girls. She glanced at me then across the room where Doug was sitting and told Carl, "Yes, I think you are right, you drive safe and don't be late."

He said, "Yes, ma'am."

I kissed Mama and said, "See you after a while" and glanced at Doug and said goodbye.

When I finally followed Carl and the other four into the kitchen, I saw the beer under Carl's arm. I told him, "You better not let my mom see that." They all laughed and said he had it with him while he was talking to my mom. I almost fell over; my mother was a stickler about alcohol. She hated the stuff, that's why she was in the den and not where we were. She knew her boys drank, but she did not like to see it. I asked Carl, "What makes you so special?"

He replied, "Your mama loves me. I go by to see her every day on my way to work."

We went in his car to go to West Ashley. I rode in the front with him and the other four crammed into to the back. We laughed all the way over there; then all at once, Carl said, "I need to stop and pulled over on the side of the road."

I thought something was wrong with the car. So Terry, Dave, and Carl got out of the car and went to the back of the car facing away from the car Nancy's friend. Cara said, "What are they doing?" And went to turn around when Nancy said, "Don't look, they are going to the bathroom."

She acted like she had never heard of that; she started to turn around again when Nancy stopped her. They guys came back around the car, and we were off again. When we dropped her off, Carl decided Dave could drive back to Goose Creek and we would ride in the back. He asked me if he could kiss me, and I told him I don't kiss guys on the first date. He said, "Okay." Then we dropped Dave off, and then it was just me and Carl in the backseat. We were talking when he pulled me close and kissed me; his eyes were twinkling, so I let him kiss me again. We went to my house and sat on the front porch and talked—Nancy, Terry, Carl, and me. We made plans to go to the beach the next day before they left. They picked us up around 11:00 a.m. as planned. Nancy and I did not plan to go swimming; we had just got our hair done the day before at the beauty shop where I was now working as a shampoo girl, a receptionist, and general helper for the stylist.

I made $.25 for every head I shampooed, and when I curled wigs and hairpieces, they paid me the same, which was good money for someone still in school. The stylist only made $3.50 for a shampoo and set.

We went to Isle of Palms beach; it was hot, but Nancy and I sat on the blanket while the guys went swimming. They just needed a reason to take their shirts off. They were hunks. Carl was very well-built and had a beautiful chest covered in silky black hair. When he turned around to come out of the water, I gasped and told Nancy, "Don't look, he is mine."

She said, "Okay, and mine's not bad either."

We went back home. Nancy had to get home early; she had to work the next day, and she knew her parents would be waiting. After everyone left, I had a shower and wondered if I would hear from Carl again that evening. I did; he called to say he needed to come and get his wallet that was in my purse. I told him I would walk outside so I could hand it to him. I was outside like I said when he rounded the corner. He pulled up on the verge of the grass. I walked over to his car and handed him his wallet and said "Have a nice evening" as I turned to go.

He asked me to stop and said, "I wish I could stay here with you."

I asked him why he could not stay. Was there a problem? He then told me he had a date with his sister-in-law's niece. I smiled and said, "Then you had better be on your way. Don't keep the girl waiting." He looked at me funny and then he asked me, "You don't mind?"

I replied, "I don't mind. I don't own you."

He said, "I don't want to go."

I said, "It's too late now to change your mind." Secretly I was glad he did not want to go, but I did not show it. I said, "You had better go. You will be late. Bye," and walked to the house.

About an hour and a half later, I was cleaning up after supper, washing dishes when there was a knock on the front door. I answered it, and there he (Carl) was, standing there on the porch. He smiled and asked if he could come in. I said, "Of course you can. What about your date?"

He replied, "She did not like my car." All I could do was laugh. You would have thought she had wrecked it because of the way he looked. He then told me, "She did not like my Mustang, so I took her back home. Now, I'm here. Do you have plans for this evening?"

I told him no. I was just going to read or listen to music. Then he wanted to know if he could listen to music with me; I told him that would be fun.

We sat and talked for a long time with the music playing in the background. I told him I had some things I needed to talk to him about; that's when I told him about Roger and my little boy.

I told him straight out, and he said he knew I had a baby and that I had given it up for adoption. That it did not bother him except he could see it weighed heavy on my heart. I told him it did, and I was dealing with it as best I could. I did not let other people know what was going on in my life. I put on a happy face every morning and faced the world. I was not like me to be unhappy or to show I was unhappy. He gathered me in his arms and just held me and told me if I wanted to be sad, sometimes I could with him. That was not likely; we liked the same music, and we liked to dance. We found plenty of things to do to keep busy.

I was out of summer school and started working on Friday and Saturday at the beauty shop. Carl called me every morning after he got up all that week. On Friday night, I was reading in my room when around 7:00 p.m., someone knocked on the front door. I answered it and there was Carl.

I said, "You are working tonight."

He just grinned and said, "I gave blood and got half the night off." He was not by himself. Terry was with him, so he asked me if I wanted to go get a soda. I told him sure. I asked him to come in and to wait a minute while I told Mama where I was going. I also needed to go make sure I looked all right. Mama said I looked fine, my hair was fine, and "Don't be too late. You have to work tomorrow."

I told her, "Yes, ma'am," grabbed my purse, and was gone. We rode around and talked to our friends at the Target Drive-in, had a soda, and then he took Terry home and then brought me back home. He asked me not to forget that I had agreed to go with him to the family reunion in Orangeburg on Sunday afternoon. I said I remembered and would be ready when he came to pick me up. He kissed me good night and asked me if I would be ready around seven o'clock tomorrow night. I told him I thought so, just depends on what time we get off work. If I was going to be late, I'd call him.

Talk about jumping in with both feet, which is what it felt like going to the family reunion. I knew his mom and dad, but then there were his siblings, Cleo and his wife Joyce, Jimmy and his fiancé Brenda, and his sister Carol and her two boys. That was okay. I knew these people and then there were his aunts and uncles. The aunts were his mothers, sisters, and they loved Carl like he was theirs. Boy did I get looked over from top to bottom, making sure I was good enough for him. I was the first girl he had ever brought to a reunion. There were lots of people there, but he took me around to be introduced to every one of them. His grandparents, his great-uncles and great-aunts and all his cousins. It was a lot of fun, and they were precious, the grandparents, great-uncles and aunts, and regular aunts and uncles. Trust me when I put the regular aunts first; it is because these ladies led the charge of everything in the family, along with Carl's mom, their big sister. Strong women who had minds of their own and said so very plainly, which was where I was to, I knew I could handle that; it was okay by me. I had no fear of anyone, I had become me take me or leave me. I was not going to get hurt again no matter what. We came back home early evening and then went to the drive-in-movies. We parked on the next to the last row; little did we know, all our friends from his school and mine were behind us. To say the least, we had fun.

Chapter 9

Carl started coming over in the mornings on Monday, Tuesday, Wednesday, and Thursday to eat breakfast with Bob (my brother); they both got up late, and I cooked breakfast for them. One morning, I was rushing around cooking while they sat at the table waiting. I forgot the biscuits were in the oven, and when I remembered they were too done, well, they can add extra butter to them and gave the biscuits to them. Bob picked his up and said, "Betty, these biscuits are hard as a rock."

I told him, "Just eat them."

Carl reached for one and agreed with him, and then they started trying to find an appropriate name for them. They ended up calling them hockey pucks. By then, I wanted to throw them at them. I let them have their little joke, but they did not get biscuits for a while. I know how to win my battles and fight back.

When we went on our third date, we doubled with his brother Jimmy and Brenda. We went to the Magnolia Drive-in in West Ashley, a community within the Charleston area. We were watching *Camelot*. I was enjoying it, but Carl was like "It's okay." He wanted to talk, so he was asking me questions, and I was listening to him and the movie at the same time. Then he asked me what I was going to do when I graduated from high school. I told him I was going to get a job and move into an apartment with Nancy. He looked at me now. I was paying attention to him, wondering why he asked me that. He leaned back into the back seat and crossed his arms.

Okay, I thought. I guess he did not like my answer. He turned his head and whispered into my ear, "If you move in with anyone, it will be me."

I said, "Excuse me."

He replied, "You heard me. I said it in plain English. We will talk about this later when we are alone."

Well, I thought, *boy you had better have a very good explanation. Nobody talks to me like that and gets away with it. Teasing is one thing, but this was not teasing and don't flex you muscles at me.* I was not going to say anything now but just wait till later.

The next weekend, we were having another party at Kline and Peggy's house again. I was still walking around Carl with a slightly different frame of mind. I was waiting for him to bring the subject of MY life after graduation back up again. He still came for breakfast, but we always had people around us, so I let it slide, waiting for him to say something. If he thought I was moving in with him; he had a hard lesson to learn not doing that. I will be married before I move in with anyone.

This party was different from all the others we had; this time, all of Carl's siblings and mutual friends were invited along with our usual group of family, cousins, and friends. They all came bringing food, drinks, and BYOB. We were dancing the night away when Carl asked me to go into the den with him. I said okay. Hey, I had three brothers outside I was not worried. The first thing he did was kiss me, and then he said, "I love You and I want you to wear my ring." Then he slid his high school ring off his finger to hand it to me. "Will you wear it please?"

I said, "I need to think about this and what it means."

He said, "I want to marry you when you graduate from school. I don't want you to live with anyone else but me. That's what I needed to say last week, but there were other people around us. I did not think you wanted me to say that in front of them."

"No, you are right. I did not want you to say anything last week. You made me nervous the way you acted, and I'm here to tell you don't ever do that to me again because I will be out of your life so fast you won't be able to see straight."

"So will you wear my ring?" he asked again.

I told him, "Yes." I would wear his ring, but we still had things to talk about and facts to get straight.

He replied, "I know, and we will as soon as possible."

When we went back into the kitchen, Wanda was sitting at the table and asked, "Did she say yes?"

Carl was standing on the stair behind me and put his arm around me and answered her, saying, "Yes, she did." He turned me around to face me and kissed me again. Then everyone knew he had asked me to marry him.

That's when everyone started partying big time; congratulations were in order, and drinks were served. I did not drink; that was not my thing. I liked my Pepsi right out of the bottle, and nothing added to it. Carl had too much to drink because he was drinking with his friends; he finally ended up on the floor of the living room and went to sleep. By then, it was late, and everyone had too much to drink.

I was inside the kitchen when my cousin Kenny and his girlfriend came in the patio doors and said, "You will have to find music from somewhere else" and started packing up his equipment. I asked him why, and he said, "Your brothers are in a fight." I thought this is bad and it was; they usually get on fine, but when you add alcohol, it is never a good thing. I went to the door and now Carl's brother Jimmy and his best friend Legrand were fighting; it was turning into a melee. The fight moved from the backyard to the side yard and then to the front yard. As I was watching from the back. I decided I would go back into the house to see if I could help Peggy, but she was out front, and Carl was still asleep on the floor and his car was being driven down the street! I went out the front door at a run and asked the first person I saw, "Who is driving Carl's car?"

Someone else told me it was Tommy he had taken Jimmy and Legrand's girlfriends for a ride to get them out of the way because they were now fighting in the middle of the street, and Kline's mailbox was standing with the door pointing to the sky.

I was upset about that, but I was also trying to find out what happened and who hit who first—Will, Kline, or Bob. Later, I got all the information I wanted from all sides. I was so glad Carl was asleep. He slept through the whole thing and woke up the next morning, which is when he learned about all of it, and he was glad he was asleep too. That was the end of the parties.

All this happened in late July, so I continued to work and see Carl in the mornings if we could arrange it. I worked on Friday mornings and then he worked Friday evenings. This went on for a while, then he decided he wanted to work first shift or days as some people call it. Just before school started, he made the change. That's when he came over every night of the week sometimes; we just sat and talked, and sometimes we would go out and meet friends. Everyone liked Carl, and we had lots of friends. My family thought he was the bee's knees; starting with my mom, she loved Carl.

I was getting ready to go back to school late August, and I had to go take my senior picture and get clothes ready and make a few things. Like I said before, I like to sew and made some dresses and skirts for school.

I did not like to wait till the last minute to know what I was wearing. I always put out my clothes the night before, so I did not have to hunt for something to wear. That way, if something needed to be ironed, I did it before I went to bed. I was usually the first person up in the mornings. I would make coffee and take Bob a cup so he would get up and go to work. Then I started getting dressed and then sometimes fix breakfast for everyone.

We dated, and I realized I did love Carl. We got more serious and started talking about marriage. We tried to keep things between us on an even keel, but it was very hard; the more we were together, the harder it got.

We took Mama to Augusta to take Christmas presents to Will and Wanda's children and for them. We love seeing them; they had moved from near us to there. We spent the whole day together. We took Mama back home, and then we went out; we should have parted company there, but we did not and that was the night I got pregnant with my son, Cleo. I sure did not think that would happen, but it did, and I found out later that month when my cycle was not regular. I made a doctor's appointment after Christmas to make sure and the rabbit died as they say. When I got back from the doctor, I went to the place where my mom worked and told her I was fine, and I brought her car back to her. Then I went next door to the garage when Carl was working on a car with Kenny, my cousin.

Carl came out from under the car and told Kenny he would be right back he was going to run me home. When we left the garage and was on our way, he asked me without any prompting what the doctor said. I had already told him my concern before I went. He pulled over on side of the road so we could talk and turned to face me, and I told him that he was going to be a father. He reached for me as his eyes filled up and told me he was glad I was okay and now we need a wedding. I can't say I was sorry either; I was really elated inside. God was going to let me have another child, which is all I could think about.

When we got to the house, Bob was at home; he was drinking coffee. Carl told him we were getting married and he said, "Good luck, I am happy for you." Then he asked me, "Does Mama know yet?"

And I said, "No, but we will tell her when she gets home."

He got up from the table and went to his room. When he came back, he was all dressed and told us, "Good luck telling Mama" and was out the door.

I said, "Where you are going?"

He replied, "Anywhere but here. Bye."

We decided to tell Mama we were getting married next week, and that was all we told her. She asked us if we were sure, and we told her we were. Then she asked me about school. Carl told her I was going to go to night school to finish.

So we were going out that weekend for New Year's Eve to a club in North Charleston with his brothers and mine with their wives and fiancés. I was looking forward to dancing with him all evening. We had just gotten our marriage license and was on top of the world.

The day before New Year's Eve, the phone rang in the kitchen while I was getting dressed, and Evelyn answered it and told me it was for me, and she did not know who it was, just a guy. I was getting dressed to go out with Carl, and I was in my slip doing my hair, so I went to answer the phone. I said "Hello," expecting one of our friends to be on the phone, but no, it was not a friend. It was Roger; his exact words were, "Do you remember the redheaded guy you use to go out with?"

I gasped and said, "Yes, I do."

He then proceeded to ask me if I would go out with him. I was stunned.

For a few seconds, I did not know how to respond, and then I told him, "No." I could not and would not go out with him that I was getting married next week.

"What do you mean you are getting married next week?"

I told him I was pregnant, and I was getting married next week. He said, "No, you are not pregnant. You had the baby."

I replied, "Yes, I had our baby, but now I am having another one."

He asked me who I was marrying, and I told him, "Carl Barrs."

He replied, "He is a nice guy."

I responded with "Yes, he is very nice."

He then asked me if he could ask me a question. I said, "Yes, go ahead and ask."

He asked me if I would tell him if I knew if the baby was a boy or a girl. I told him that he had a son out there in the world, and I hoped he never got to see him. In my heart, I knew I was being mean, but I could not help myself. There was a knock on the front door, and when my cousin Jan answered the door, it was Carl, and I was not ready. I told Roger I needed to go, and he said, "Just a minute, please."

Carl went into the kitchen where Evelyn and Jan were. I heard him ask them who I was talking to when Evelyn replied, "Some guy." He did not come into the hall where I was, thank goodness. I was not ready for that. Roger told me he wished me well and thanked me for talking to him, and then he said goodbye. I got up off the floor I was sitting on and went to hang up the phone that I slammed down around the corner and said to the room in general, "I've got to finish getting dressed."

I heard Carl call my name, but I ran to my room to grab my robe. I was not ready to see him. I was shaking so bad, and I was ready to cry it was all too much. I needed time to digest what had just happened. Carl knocked on my bedroom door and asked me if he could come in and I told him, "I would be right there." I went to the door, and he said, "Who has upset you? Was it, Doug?"

I replied, "No, it was not Doug."

He went to ask me something else when he looked like a light bulb went off in his brain, and he swore and said, "I know who it was. I am going to get your brothers and we will finish the job they never did." He turned and went down the hall and out the front door. I was right behind him, and after we got outside, me on the porch and him at the bottom of the steps, I said, "Carl, if you leave here, don't ever come back because I will not be here and neither will this baby."

He turned on a dime and said, "What do you mean?"

I said, "I have already had my name dragged through the mud in this town, and once was enough. I will get on the first bus I can no matter where it is going, and the baby and I will disappear."

He said, "You don't mean that."

So I asked him, "Are you going to put me to the test?"

He came back to the porch and said, "No, because I can see you mean it."

I said, "I'll go finish getting dressed. Will you still be here?"

He said, "Yes, I'll wait on you we need to talk some more."

Chapter 10

We were married on Friday, January 9, 1970. We were so happy; things worked out perfectly for us. We got married in Kline and Peggy's den. We had a white trellis covered with greenery; it looked lovely. Carl's best man was Cleo, his oldest brother; my bridesmaid was Evelyn, my little sister; and my brother, Kline, gave me away. We felt like we were walking on a cloud; everything seemed to fall in to place. Earlier that week, a neighbor lady that I babysat for told us about a furnished apartment for rent, and we rented it. It was close to Carl's work. So we were set, it had just about everything we needed and what we did not have our mothers helped us out. The only fly in the ointment was, I had not told my mother I was pregnant yet, and it worried me a lot. I did not like to be like that.

After having my earlier baby, my mom and I had become really good friends. I felt so ashamed of hiding this from her. I knew she would love me regardless, but still, it bothered me.

I was completely happy. I loved Carl and I know he loved me; the wedding was nice with some of the family there, and I had all the things a girl needs at her wedding—something old, something new, something borrowed, and something blue. The something borrowed was a pair of gloves I got from Bonnie, my big sister.

She said, "Wear these with your beige dress." I would not let myself wear white because I felt tarnished and was not brash enough to go that route. Because I had cut the end of my thumb off on my right hand in a fan motor that ran the water pump at my aunt and uncle's house when I was two, I wanted to cover my hands. I told her I did not want to take them off when he put my ring on. She said, "I can fix that." She went to her sewing box and got her scissors out and took the left glove and cut the wedding band finger off the glove. I also had a new dress and old shoes that I had, and the blue was unmentionables.

After the ceremony, we had wedding cake, nuts and mints, and punch. We stayed for a while, talking and being congratulated by our family and friends. Carl kept asking me, "Can we go now?"

And I kept saying, "In a few minutes, we can't be rude," and he would growl in my ear. Finally, I said to everyone, "We have to go we need to stop at the grocery store and get milk for breakfast."

Everyone laughed, and there were comments like "We understand" and "Sure, you do," "No problem. Ya'll have fun now." Then our friends started and out the door we went after kissing our mothers good night.

I started to night school the next week, and I got a new job working at Rodenberg's grocery warehouse as a receptionist. That worked out well. I took Carl to work and came back home, got dressed, and went to work. He got a ride home when I got off work. I went home to fix us something to eat, and three nights a week, I went to school from 7:00 to 9:00 p.m. We were always busy going about life, the way we were supposed to be doing.

I went to my mom's one night about a month after we got married for a visit. I was there a lot, but this night was different. She was in the kitchen drying dishes, and I asked her if she needed help. She said, "No, but I want to talk to you."

I knew she knew my secret, and she did. She came right after me; she said, "Are you pregnant?"

I told her, "Yes, I am."

She looked at me like she could spit nails and said, "What kind of example are you setting for your little sister? This is twice now. I'm very disappointed in you," she added.

I was heartbroken, but I replied, "I did not know I had to live my life to set an example for Evelyn. She can live her own life." She was not happy with me, so I told her, "I have to go. I'll be late for school. Bye."

That was the first time that I left my mother's house without kissing her goodbye in a very long time. I went to school; it was hard sitting there when all I wanted to do was cry, but I stayed and went to pick up Carl at his parents' house when I got out so we could go home.

Carl knew immediately there was something wrong. I was in the driver's seat and did not get out; he was on the carport talking to Jimmy, his brother. He came over to the car and opened the door for me and said, "I'll drive." I got out and walked around the car and got in the passenger seat while he went and told Jimmy we had to go we both had to go to work in the morning. After he got into the car and pulled out of the driveway, he asked me, "What has happened? Who has upset you?"

I started crying. I felt awful; disappointing my mama was not something I took lightly, but it was my fault, and I knew it. Again, Carl Asked me why I was crying. I told him, "Mama knows I am pregnant."

He turned to look at me and said, "We are pregnant. What else did she say?"

I repeated the conversation to him and how I left and went to school. He reminded me, "This is not like last time. You are now a married woman, and we are having a baby we will both love and care for. What are you going to do about your mother?" he asked me.

I told him nothing. I was just going to continue working and going to school. I was not going back over there for a while. He asked me, "If that was a good idea, you and your mother are very close."

I told him, "I don't know what else to do. I can't go back there right now," sobbing all the time.

He also told me, "You need to stop crying you are only going to make yourself sick. Your morning sickness already wears you down. Remember, I love you and always will."

He was so sweet, and he just made me love him more. When we got home, he ran me a bath and told me go soak. I pulled myself together while I was soaking, and I did not go back to Mama's for a little while.

Mama called me two weeks later and asked me if I was going to come and see her, I replied, "Yes, ma'am."

"This weekend," she asked, and I replied again, "Yes, ma'am, we will see you Friday night after work."

She told me, "Come for dinner."
I told her, "Thank you, I love you, Mama."
She replied, "I love you too, don't ever forget that."
I told her, "Yes, ma'am, I know, bye."

On Friday night, we went to Mama's. I was so glad to see her; she hugged me as tight as I hugged her. My heart felt so much better. GOD does wonderful things in our lives, and you learn no one on the face of this Earth loves you like your Mama. We had dinner with Evelyn and Mama, and everything was fine. I didn't want to ever be at odds with her again. I went back to her house on Saturday so we could go shopping.

We stayed in the apartment until I was four months pregnant. I had to go to the doctor. I started having problems. I was treating a miscarriage, so we moved to Goose Creek into a house Carl's daddy owned; it was one-half block from his parents' house, and I did not have to climb stairs. His dad went shopping and bought us a bedroom suite, a dinette table and chairs, and a living room suite. We had a TV that my mom had given us, and we had pots pans and dishes from our wedding shower. Shortly after that, I had to quit work and stay home. I sewed and made things ready for the baby and myself.

Our son, Cleo Vinson Barrs, was born on August 18, 1970. I was so happy; he was beautiful, and we thought he was the best baby in the world. He was smart, funny, and his own person right away. His personality was special; he was such a loving child, and he was mine. As Cleo grew, I wondered how his brother was doing; he was never far from my mind. I would hug Cleo and pray for my oldest son. Did I mention my mother thought Cleo was the cat's meow? In other words, she thought he was fabulous. I went back to work and Bonnie kept Cleo for me until I came home and heard him call her Mama that was it; my baby was not calling anybody but me Mama. We tried to let someone else keep him, but that didn't work either. I quit work and stayed home until he was two years old and knew who Mama was.

When Cleo was almost five and getting ready to go to kindergarten, I got pregnant again. Not only was I pregnant, a whole bunch of us in the family were expecting. Evelyn was due in January, Nancy was due in early February, it was due at the end of February, Tina was due in June, and Brenda was due in September. We had five new babies coming to our family; it was wonderful.

Our beautiful baby girl, Lori Lee Barrs, was born February 24, 1976. It was America's Bicentennial! How I wanted a girl and GOD gave me one. We were so happy. We felt our family was complete because I had so much trouble carrying Cleo and Lori, the doctor tied my tubes the next day after Lori was born.

We had a good life; the children were healthy. We were happy; we always had what we needed. Carl loved his children like no man I had ever seen. I'm sure you have noticed I have not mention, my father; he committed suicide when I was thirteen years old; he was a very sick man, and he was a very mean man. He was what my mom called a street angel and a house devil. Anyone that knew him on the outside thought he was wonderful until they found out how he treated my mom and the seven of us children. We realized later he was very ill; he was either bipolar or manic depressive, never on an even keel. It made life hard for all of us, but GOD gave us a saving grace, our mother. So seeing Carl play with and love his children was a joy for me. I loved him so much for that.

Chapter 11

In February 1989, my mother told me that my son that I gave up for adoption had come to her house, and he told her his name was Jeremy Anderson. She also said, "I looked him up in the phone book and this is the address in West Ashley." I was in shock and terrified at the same time; finally, I would get to meet him. What would he think of me because I gave him away? She also said he had also come in 1986, but she did not tell me because I was sick at the time. She had told Bonnie, and they agreed not to tell me. I was having serious headaches then; they even thought I had a stroke until they did a CAT scan. The headaches were caused by my sinuses, and because I had migraines for years. I had just started going to a new doctor who told me I was addicted to the medicine the other doctors had given me. I had to be weaned off the Valium and pain meds, and he changed my blood pressure meds; that way, I could have sinus surgery. After I had the surgery, I did not have any more headaches, so in 1989, I was fine. Now I got the information that I needed.

I went home and told Carl all about it; he told me to get busy looking. He also said, "If I can help, let me know." I immediately started looking. First, I called the number for the address she had given me, and there was not a Jeremy Anderson living in the apartment complex. I then decided to go downtown to the courthouse to search the court records. I found out quickly how to read the record books; they were big, oversized journals, and all the entries had been handwritten. I copied down all the entries for boys that my attorney had done from the time my baby was born until he was about two. There was no Jeremy Andersons, but a couple of the boys had Jeremy as a middle name, so I was hopeful.

The next thing I did was call Roger at his home in Maine to let him know what I was doing and to give him the information I had been given. He wanted to also talk to my mother and get the story from her, so I called her and asked if she would talk to him. She was fine with that, so he called Mama, and she told him just what she told me. She also told me that my oldest son looked more like me than my other children. Roger called me back and told me he had talked to her, and he was satisfied with the information.

I later joined an organization called Triad; the people in the organization taught you how to search for a loved one. What to say and what other organizations that were out there to help you with your inquires. I traveled back and forth to the state capital Columbia, once a month for these meetings. I also hired a private investigator to help me look; they did not have any luck either.

Later that year, on early September, my mother went to stay at her sister's house in Darlington, South Carolina, for a week. Ken brought her home, and he noticed there was something wrong with Mama. She was not aware of her surroundings, and she asked him over and over where they were going. I cannot tell you how many times she had been on that road in the last twenty-five years. He got her home and told us what had happened, so we kept an eye on her.

A few weeks later in September, we had to get ready for a huge hurricane. It was off the coast and coming straight for Charleston; we knew it was going to be bad we prepared as best we could for that kind of thing. Kline took Mama, Evelyn, and her family to his house. Evelyn and Otto were building a new house, and they had sold theirs. We all came through the Hurricane Hugo without much damage, thank the LORD.

After that, we really noticed sometimes Mama was not the same. Bonnie and I took her to the doctor, and he sent her to a neurologist. The neurologist told us she was in the first stages of Alzheimer disease; we were expecting that, but it was still devasting news. Mama was a smart woman; she had graduated as salutatorian when she graduated from Summerville High School in 1935. She was an avid reader too. We did not tell her what the doctor said, but I found a book at her house on Alzheimer that she read. One evening, she got upset and I had to medicate her, and she told me she would rather die than lose her mind. I understood what she was saying because she was a strong woman too, and her worst fear was losing her dignity and her mind. She usually stayed with me at my house at night because she had started having sundowners, and she needed to be with someone in the evenings.

I called her on November 2, 1991, in the evening so I could pick her up and take her home with me, but she told me no she was sleepy and was going to bed. I then told her I would stay with her, and again she told me no, that she was all right, to go home and be with my family. I tried to get her to let one of my children, who were sixteen and twenty-one, come and stay, and again she said no. Like I said, she was a strong woman, and I could only ask; she was my mother.

The next morning, I called, and she did not answer. I was not worried; she had probably gone to church with someone in the family. Later when I called and she did not answer, I went to her house; the glass screen door was locked, so I went across the street to the Smith's house and asked Bubba and Winnie if I could use their phone to call Carl to come help me with the door. I went back across the street, and this time, I pulled on the glass door it came open. I noticed that Uncle Bubba had followed me across the street. I went down the hall calling her name; when I got to her room, the bed was made and she was not there. I turned and went back down the hall, calling her name. I went to the den and laundry room, and no Mama. Then I checked the backyard; her dog was there, but Mama was not there. I went back down the hall and realized the bathroom door was only partially open. As I went to open the door, I heard Carl's footstep on the threshold of the front door. I pushed the door, and it would not open all the way. I looked around the door, and there she was, lying on the floor.

I screamed "Mama!" and went into the bathroom and got down on the floor and picked her up. I knew she was dead; her mouth was turning blue, and she was not breathing. Carl came into the bathroom, and he confirmed my fears; yes, she was dead. No hope—there was none to be had; after a few minutes, he asked me to put her back on the floor because we should not move her. I did not want to let her go. He told me we have people to call, so I had to get off the floor. I went to Mama's bedroom and sat on the bed while Carl dialed Bonnie's number. I told her she needed to come to Mama's house and that Mama was dead. Uncle Bubba told Carl to tell Bonnie to call EMS from her house because she lived in the city and we were in the county; the city would get here quicker. I went back to the bathroom. I had to go back in there and wait for whomever came first.

The ambulance came really quick, once they got there, they did not want anyone to go into the bathroom. I had to explain to them that my mother had seven children, and for their own safety, they had better get out of the way when the wanted to go in there. They all started arriving: Bonnie and Spencer, Kline and Kim, Bob and Karen, and then Evelyn and Otto. Evelyn and Otto got there last, and when she went to go into the bathroom, this young woman from EMS told her no. I heard Evelyn say, "I'm going in, so get out of my way." I told the young lady to move and to do it now. "That is my mama's baby," so let her in and she did.

The coroner came, and I had to sit with him and answer all the questions he had to ask because I had found her; you never think of things like that until you experience them. When he got through, he asked me if there was anything else he could do for me. I asked him to please get my mother off the floor. He said they were waiting for the funeral home to come and get her, and I told him no; the ambulance is here, to let them take her there now. He said that they could do that, and I thanked him for his consideration.

By then, most of my siblings and their families were there. Carl had called Cleo and Lori, and they had arrived. We were waiting for Will, who lived in Augusta, Georgia, and Ken and his family that lived in Lumberton, North Carolina. Our aunts and uncles and cousins were there, and food was coming in the door from friends and family. This was one gathering I had never wanted to attend. We stayed together until all the siblings were there. I was hard on all of us if there was one person; we all loved it was Mama.

When Mama had her heart attack and fell, she bruised her head so some in the family decided to keep her casket closed for the viewing. When I got to the funeral home and saw that, I left the room and refused to go back in there. I held up pretty good that night I was so mad I could have hurt someone, but my best friend Melinda was there to keep me calm. She sat with me in the hall until it was time to go. All my family was in that room, and I guess they did not miss me, but that's okay. I always manage to get through whatever GOD gives me. I went home and sat in the bathtub and cried, and I told Carl I was not going to the funeral unless that casket was opened, and I saw my mama before they put her in the ground. He called Bonnie and told her they had to open the casket the next morning before the funeral so I could see Mama.

I had picked the clothes she had on. I picked out the casket, and I was her caretaker when she needed me. I was going to see her and that was that.

Once we got to the cemetery, I was close to completely freaking out. I told Carl, "Please let me just die and be buried with her. I could not live if she was gone."

He told me that I had him and two children that loved me too, and they needed me like I needed her, and we would all get better as time went on.

We got through the funeral without any more hitches, and we continued our lives, but twenty-one days later was my fortieth birthday. I went to Mama's house, made myself some coffee, and sat there and cried all day long. The person that loved me the most in the world was gone, and I wanted to be gone too. I worked really hard to come out of my depression and did good until it was time to put up my Christmas tree. I always helped Mama do hers, and it just made it worse that I could not help her or help her make her gift list and take her shopping. We always enjoyed doing that and going to lunch. Gradually, I got better and was working again, but I never stopped missing her.

Chapter 12

The week before our twenty-third anniversary, Carl called me from work and told me he was feeling bad, and I told him to take a Nitrostat, and I would come and take him to the doctor. He told me he did not have any Nitrostat, and he had already went to the pharmacy to get some, and they did not have any; there was a shortage at that time. So I told him to call his cardiologist and talk to him, and I would come there to get him. He worked in Mt. Pleasant and had rode to work with his sister. While he was doing that, I went and got Lori out of school so she could work in my place at the bookstore. Then I went to his work to pick him up. When he got in the car, he told me the doctor was waiting for him at Roper Hospital Emergency Room.

We were off in a hurry him and his Pepsi and me scared to death; he was going to die before I got him there. Finally, we were there, and when we walked in, he sat down, and I went to the desk to tell them who he was. The receptionist picked up her handheld walkie-talkie and said, "Mr. Barrs is here now, STAT."

I turned to look at Carl; they were in the waiting room with a gurney and she was showing them who he was. She told me told me to wait I needed to fill out some papers and the doctor would come out here to talk to me when he was finished.

Dr. Grayson, Carl's cardiologist, came out and sat down beside me and said, "We are keeping him. The left side of his heart has shut down and only the small feeder veins are keeping him alive. He will have to have a heart catherization and then the surgeons will decide what is next." He then said, "You got him just in time." I was thanking God for that. My Lord is always there when I need him.

Two days later, they did the heart catherization, and the three surgeons came to see us. He had three blockages in his heart and was going to need open-heart surgery. They were going to do it in three days because they did not want to do emergency surgery on him; therefore, he would need to stay in the hospital so they could watch him and continue his medicine. The day of his surgery came, and his family and mine were there. We were all praying he would be okay; it took a lot longer than they expected, but as soon as the surgeons came to tell us he was in recovery and that he was stable, Carl's parents and his aunts and family went home. Bonnie and Evelyn stayed with me. WE were waiting to go in and see him. We had an unexpected visitor; it was the anesthesiologist. He came and sat with us to explain the delay the surgeons had not explained while everyone was there, including our children and Carl's parents.

He told us the delay was because Carl had died three separate times during the operation, once when they were putting him on the bypass machine, once during the surgery, and once when they were taking him off the bypass machine. We were astounded to hear all this and so grateful to GOD that it was not his time. We were at the hospital until the last week in January. His doctor caught me in the hall one day and told me that if Carl did everything they wanted him to do he would live five to seven years, and if he did, he would need another surgery as time went on; there was a blocked artery in the back of his heart that they could not get to, and it would need to be looked at often. I kept waiting for them to tell Carl these things, and they never did. I think they thought his cardiologist would fill him in and he would be okay. They did not know the Carl I knew; it was not long when he started not going to the doctor and then he started smoking again, which I figured was a death sentence. I told him everything the doctors told me, and he still did not quit.

I knew I was living with a time bomb; he asked me to go and buy him a pack of cigarettes one day when he was helping my cousin work on his roof. I looked at him and told him he was going to die and leave me alone. I was so angry that he did not care if I would be alone. Here we were in the best years of our lives and our children grown, and we could spend time together alone and he was not hearing me. I could feel myself becoming resentful. I still loved him and still cooked what he needed to eat and did all the thing I always did, but nothing changed until Lori told us she was going to have a baby. I thought finally he will listen. I know he wants to be a granddaddy; he will change now. The first thing I did was tell everyone, even him, "If you are going to smoke, you will do it on the back porch." I knew he would hate that and maybe it would help him quit, but it did not.

Lori had Wesley Vinson Barrs on January 23, 1998; he was a month early, and he was very small with breathing problems. When we brought him home, he still had an IV in the top of his forehead and a nurse came to the house twice a day to give him medicine. The third day was a disaster; we had a different nurse, and she told Lori she needed to come and learn how to do what she was doing. Lori started crying, handed me the baby, and ran to the bathroom. I looked at my friend that was there and said it is awfully bad when someone gets paid for a job and wants to pawn it off on someone else. I was continuing to hold Wesley when the nurse turned and said to me the only other thing to do is to call his pediatrician and put him back in the hospital. I looked at her and told her there is the phone on the wall. "Do you need me to give you the number?"

She came over to the phone and said, "No, ma'am. I have it," and proceeded to call his doctor. After she got off the phone, she gave me the information Lori needed and left; *Good riddance* was all I thought.

I took Lori and Wesley back to the hospital. Lori had to stay to she got to rest, feed, and change Wesley and the nurses gave him his medicine. It was good for Wesley and for Lori; she needed to bond with Wesley. She was not able to go to the nursery to see him the first two days, and I was the only one who got to touch him. Having him in the room with her was the best thing. I was completely in love with my new grandson and so was Carl. After Wesley was two or three weeks old, Lori went back to work. I kept Wesley and was loving it. Carl would come home from work, and when he came in the back door, he knew he was supposed to be quiet, but no, he always made noise so if Wesley was asleep, he would wake up, and he could hold him. It was so funny him trying to look sheepish as if he did not mean to do it, but I knew, and he knew I knew.

Cleo and Lori had grown up being spoiled by their daddy; he tried to get them whatever they really wanted, but he also made them work too. They learned from him that everyone in this life had to work at something to survive and to be a good human being. Most of our married life, he worked two jobs because he liked to play, and for him to do that, he had to have extra money, so he worked part time doing other things.

He worked at the gas station when they were rationing gas in the seventies. He installed wood floors in new built houses, and then he had a lawn service in the afternoons. It was September 28, 1998, Carl, Lori, Wesley, our eight-month-old grandson and myself had just finished dinner. Carl asked me to find out what time the Braves were playing baseball that night; he was going to go and sharpen the lawnmower blade and come back into the house and have a shower. Lori started cleaning the kitchen. Wesley was in the playpen playing. I went to see what time the game was. Then, the doorbell was ringing like crazy; we had a sign on the door not to ring the doorbell. It said, DO NOT RING THE DOORBELL, BABY SLEEPING. I ran to the door and Lori was right behind me; the lady next door told us Carl had fallen in the backyard.

Lori ran for the back door, and I went to the phone to call EMS. Our neighbor had come in as Lori turned to go outside when I finished talking to EMS. I told her to watch the baby while I went outside. When I got outside, Lori was on the ground screaming at her daddy to wake up. I asked her what if anything he had said; she told me he told her he was sleeping. I got down on the ground and Lori went to call Cleo while she was gone. I determined that he was dead. I listened for a heartbeat, and there was not one, and he was not breathing and the cut he got on his head he had sustained when he fell was not bleeding anymore. Our neighbor and friend Mike from across the street came running over to see what was wrong. When he saw Carl, he ran back across the street to get the dental hygienist that lived next door to him so she could perform CPR on Carl. She worked very hard and continued until EMS arrived, and by then, Cleo was there. They did all the things they have to do, but in my heart, I knew he was dead.

They put him in the ambulance, and then they were on their way to the hospital. Cleo had to go get Amy. She was five months pregnant with my granddaughter. Mike told me he would drive us to the hospital. I said, "Thanks, I'll be ready shortly." Paula, Mike's wife pulled into her driveway and came over to the house. When she heard about Carl, she said, "Go ahead. I will get Wesley and take him to my house. Thank goodness for her. I had left the neighbor in the house with him. Lori had been in and out of the house, but she had stayed with the baby. She was a GOD-send. I stopped long enough to call Carl's parents and told them what had happened. When we got to the hospital, all I remember was the emergency room being dark and Lori telling me the nurse wants us to go to this room in the far corner. I told Lori I did not want to go into that room.

She said, "Come on, Mama, it will be okay," but I knew better. When we went in, Carl's daddy, Mr. Barrs, and Carl's oldest brother, Cleo, were already there in the room. We went in and talked about how it had happened and what was done. They told me the doctors were working on him, and he would be all right. I did not respond. They did not need me to tell them what I already knew. I decided I would let the doctors do that. Cleo and Amy arrived, and the chaplain of the hospital came into the room to tell us the doctors were still working on him. I knew when he left that when he returned the doctors would be with him bring the bad news. Other people showed up, but I can't tell you who I was sitting there, waiting for the doctors to give us the blow that I knew was coming, and all I needed at that moment were my children. They were there with me, and so we waited. Shortly, the doctor and the chaplain came back into the room. Carl's daddy immediately stood up, and the doctor was walking toward me, so I got up and went to stand by Carl's daddy. He more than me needed the respect due him from the doctors. He had loved and raised this man, and I wanted him to hear what they said. The doctor told us they had done everything humanly possible to save Carl, but it was not enough. He then asked me if I would like to see Carl, and I said yes, then I asked Carl's dad if he wanted to come too, and he told me no he had to go home and tell Hannah Mae, Carl's mother, that her baby was dead.

    I asked Cleo and Lori if they wanted to see their daddy, and they told me yes; we followed the doctor back into the emergency room where they had worked on him. The doctor explained that he was still hooked up to machines and things so we would know what to expect. When I got there beside him, I think I lost my mind for a short while. All I remember is telling him I knew he was going to die and leave me, and he was not supposed to do that. Lori later told me I had climbed up on top of him and was screaming into his face and Cleo had to get me down. I honestly did not remember any of that. When I left the room, most of my and brothers and sisters where there. When a doctor and a nurse followed me out of the ER to the car and asked if they could speak to me, I said, "Of course." They said we noticed Mr. Barrs had just had a tooth pulled and if I need any information for an attorney. I understood what they were saying. Had Carl had the medication he needed before his tooth was pulled, if not there were legal ramifications. They were offering to make sure I got all the help I needed. It was a wonderful thought, but I had to explain to them I had told Carl he needed an antibiotic before he had his tooth pulled, and he told me he was getting it pulled regardless. He did not take any medicine, and I was hoping he would tell someone, and they would tell him to come back, but no, he had it pulled and that was that. I also told them I was not going after the dentist because Carl was aware, and he played Russian roulette with his life. And besides, you die when the LORD says it is your time. I have complete faith in my GOD, and if he numbers the hair on your head, surely, he numbers your days.

    I told my family what they said and then told them not to tell anyone it was my decision, and I had made it. I then told them I was going to see Carl's mother before I went back home. I knew they were all going to my house; they would not ever leave me at a time like this, and they did not. They told me they would be there when I got there.

    I went into Carl's parents and hugged his daddy. So I said, "What did you eat?" and went in and sat at Hannah Mae's feet and put my head on her knee; she looked hollow-eyed and shocked. I think by then I was less, so I had longer to come to grips with it and had been expecting it in my own way for months. You can't dismiss what the doctors say and expect to continue on as though nothing was wrong.

The Sunday before he died, I cooked supper because Cleo and Amy were coming back from Illinois where they had gone to visit her father. When I told him dinner was ready, he told me he was not hungry. I knew why he went to his mother's house at a quarter to five o'clock. I should have paid attention to what time it was when he left. His aunt Jenny was there, and I knew she was cooking. She did every night since Hannah had come out of rehab for her knee. I asked him, "What did you eat at your Mama's?"

At first he said, "I did not eat anything," and then I laughed and said, "You may as well tell me. I can call and find out." He smiled and said, "Aunt Jenny made him chicken gizzards, mashed potatoes, and gravy."

I told him, "You are not supposed to eat fried food."

He then told me, "It was delicious," and I said, "Yeah right."

That was his attitude about eating things he should not eat. I had stopped frying chicken and other things years ago when he had his heart surgery, so he went to his mama's. He was her baby, and she gave him what he wanted. Both of his parents spoiled him.

Chapter 13

When I left the Barrs' house and got to my house, my siblings and my cousins were there, so were my aunts and friends from all over. Word travels fast when something like this happens in our family; it's almost like we have drums to send the messages. I knew the telephone lines were hot. I expected nothing less. They all gathered around me and my children wanting to do whatever they could.

I had to finally sneak away and call Bruce, the husband of my best friend Melinda; she was in Florida visiting her aunt, and I did not have the number where she was. Bruce told me he would call her and let her know, but they were in a hurricane, so he did not know when she would get back home. I told him thank-you and waited. I knew she would call as soon as she got word, and she did and told me she would be there ASAP.

My brother Ken, who was a minister, was on his way, and I was waiting for him to get there. I knew I could depend on him to guide me through what I needed to do. People were asking me questions like When, where and who was doing the funeral, I told them I needed to discuss it with Ken and then I would tell them. Ken and I were always close, and I had a dilemma, ordinarily the funeral would be in two days but that was not going to happen this time because in two days was Ken's birthday and I was not having him preach his brother-in-law's funeral on his birthday.

Bonnie, Evelyn and Ken spent the night at my house. I still don't know why we went to bed. I could not sleep, and when I got out of bed, they followed me. If it had not been so sad, it would have been funny. They kept telling me I needed to sleep, and I just could not sleep. Finally, in the wee hours, we all got a little bit of sleep. Then it was time for Wesley to eat, and he let everyone know it. I got up and started the coffee. The day began with Ken and I going over what I had to do, then we collaborated on the procedure. I had my list, and he had his. GOD bless him. He went back home to have his birthday with his family and to come back with his family for the funeral on October 1.

I had to go to the funeral home and then to the cemetery where we had bought plots, only to be told they could not bury him where we had bought the plots because his casket would not fit. He was a big man, and they said he needed a bigger casket. I had to walk around the cemetery and pick another spot. It was cold and wet, and I had surgery on both my feet eighteen months earlier and still used a wheelchair and a cane when needed. But in the end, he did not need a bigger casket; he fit in a regular casket, but we did bury him in the new spot.

The funeral was just what I expected. Ken did a marvelous job; he knew all the right things to say. Carl's parents were so thankful that he did the service. I already knew what I was getting. Ken had preached part of our mama's funeral. He left you feeling wonderful about the person but assured you, you would see that loved one again if you believed in JESUS. Carl was a believer, so we all knew he was saved. Some might not have thought so, but he was.

I'll always thank GOD for the wonderful father he gave my children, and the wonderful husband I had. It took years to get pass this period of my life, but I stayed busy the first six or eight months. I kept Wesley and what a joy he was; he was a happy baby and I loved being with him. Cleo and Amy's daughter, Chelsea Ann, came on December 1, 1998. Carl would have loved her too; he was one of those men that liked babies and knew how to make them smile.

Later, Lori put Wesley in daycare, and I had to adjust to that; sometimes, I would go and get him early, so I could play with him and take him to the park. I stayed busy Melinda and Bruce were building a house, and I was helping her reupholstery some furniture. I would sew, and she would run after Wesley. We got it all done before she moved to her new house.

We spent a lot of time together, either at my house of hers; we enjoyed each other's company, and then she had to move to

Columbia. I was so sorry to see her go, after losing Mama and then Carl, she was the one person I spent most of my time with; it was truly heart-wrenching for me to see her go.

Lori decided she was going to move to Jacksonville. I was scared for her, and she was taking Wesley. I did not think I would survive that, but I adjusted. I went there at least once a month and sometimes twice. It did not last long like six months. I went to the daycare to pick up Wesley one Friday when I got there early, so I could get him ready to go eat dinner with his mom. I walked into the day care and ask to pick up Wesley and they said okay and went and got him. He was glad to see me, but I was not glad to see him; they just let me walk out the door with him. I was shaking so bad I could not believe it. They did not ask for my driving license or any proof of who I was. I turned around and went back in and told them I was appalled at what they had done. I could not believe they just causally hand children over to anyone. They had no way of knowing if I was who I said I was. To top that off, I had to clean Wesley up from head to toe. They did not wash his face and hands, and being a towhead, he was a dirt magnet. Even his diaper was dirty.

I went to Lori's work to pick her up, and I was still shaking. When she asked me what was wrong, I almost took her head off, so I told her I was taking Wesley home with me until she found a new daycare or came back home. His life was in jeopardy in that place, and I did not like it. She agreed, thank goodness, and she did come home later. She had no clue that they would just give him to me she was appalled too.

After being home for a while, she moved in with her cousin Julie; she is my sister Bonnie's youngest daughter. Julie is like one of my children; she was always at my house. I love her like she is mine.

When things became normal, I started looking for a church that I wanted to belong to. I went to the Seventh-Day Adventist Church while growing up with my parents, then the Baptist Church with Carl. I wanted to go to a church that made me feel at home. I never had felt that way after I was grown now that I am over forty; it was my choice. I wanted GOD in my life like never before, and I think I felt that way because people usually do not put GOD in first place. I wanted to go regularly, I wanted to participate, and I want to tithe on all my money. I wanted to be in a family of believers. I was looking but had not found one.

My friend Carolyn Davidson, the author of some of the Harlequin Historical, called and asked me if I would follow her to the car dealership and pick her up when she dropped her car off. I told her of course I would. We went early so she suggested we go to breakfast. I was so ready breakfast is my favorite meal. We went to a hometown restaurant called Alex's. They made the best breakfast in town. While we were there, a man came over to talk to Carolyn, and she introduced me to him. He was her pastor at her church that was right around the corner from my house, The Nazarene Church; he was so nice. I knew I wanted to hear him preach, and he invited me to their church. I told them both I would think about it, but I knew I was going to go.

Then Bonnie fell and broke her knee, and I went to her house to live with her and her husband Karl while she mended. As she got better, I started going to church on Sundays because Karl was home with her.

When I got back home, I decided to do what GOD wanted me to do, jump into this church with both feet. I was home, and I knew it right away. They welcomed me with open arms and treated me like family. What a thrilling feeling; it draws you so close to GOD when you feel like that.

I was going to church three times a week; it made a definite change in my life. I went to church for a guest speaker that was unable to come. Dr. Lindsay was preaching, and the HOLY SPIRIT grabbed hold of me and changed my life in a major way. Dr. Lindsay was preaching about Adam and Eve in the garden of Eden, and this is what happened as he was speaking. The LORD was walking in the garden in the late afternoon and called to Adam and Eve, "Where are you?" At that moment, all I could see was me standing behind a tree in the garden of Eden smoking a cigarette. I was horrified. I knew when he made an altar call, I was going to go and give the LORD my sin. I did just that. I went to the altar and my friends and Dr. Lindsay prayed with me; it was wonderful. I felt the HOLY SPIRIT telling me it was okay. I had won this battle. I felt as though I was that much closer to my LORD.

After church, I was going to go and eat with my friend Sherry. She told me GOD does not expect you to quit cold turkey and I told her, "Yes, he did, and HE had died on that cross to save me. How could I do anything that would hurt HIM?" I told her, "No, I would never smoke again." I got rid of my cigarettes and that was the end of my smoking. When we rely on GOD to help us with something, HE will and in a way we never expect. What a glorious FATHER, SON, and HOLY SPIRIT we have.

For the first time in my life, I was able to pay tithe like I was supposed to, and I did the first of the month every month. One day, I was sitting at my computer writing checks paying tithe and my bills when I stopped to thank GOD that I had enough money to pay them all and have money for food and gas when GOD spoke to me in my mind and told me if you gave more you would have more. I told HIM out loud, "Okay, GOD, that's what I am going to do." When I did give more than the 10 percent, I was giving it worked. I don't have a clue how. except I had unshakable faith, and my GOD did what he said. When I see GOD working in my life like that it makes me sad to think about the times. I did not live like that. But no matter who is in my life my GOD and the LORD JESUS CHRIST comes first.

As time went on, I traveled with my friend Carolyn and her husband and his cousin back and forth to Michigan to see their children, and we went on trips for her book signings. We went to Texas, Alabama, and Florida with all the states in between. Once we drove to Michigan by way of US Highway 52. It went from Charleston, South Carolina, to Michigan. It was okay, but there are no rest stops on that road; you need to find yourselves bathrooms. I'd rather drive the interstate. When you make that trip, you understand why they built the interstate highways.

We went to Michigan one time by way of New York so Carolyn could go and see her agent who was a very nice lady. From there, we went to Niagara Falls, then we went to Canada and then back into the United States in Michigan.

We all had a wonderful time; we got to the hotel in Canada where we stayed the night, and they found out that Carolyn was a writer with at least twenty or so books; they had her sign the book that they had presidents and heads of states sign. We went out for dinner, and when we got back, they brought us dessert and champagne. What fun that was; we all took a taste and decided it was not for us. We did not like it; we settled for water, soda, or coffee with our dessert.

Chapter 14

Lori told me she was going to have another baby; well, this is how it happened. Sherry and I had gone to the store to pick up some items, and when we came back, Julie's car was at my house, and I wondered why because it was late, and she should be home. We went into the house, and Julie got up to hug me and Lori said, "Mama, I have to tell you something." I looked at her and said, "If you are going to tell me you are pregnant, don't."

She replied, "But I have to. I'm almost six months.' The reason I did not know was because she was a big girl, and she hid it well.

I went straight to my room and shut and locked the door. I needed help with this, and I knew where to get it. I needed to pray. I asked God to help me be civil about this. I was not going to throw stones. I would not and could not I had done the same thing at fifteen and eighteen but not at twenty-two and twenty-six years old. Finally, after spending time in prayer with the Lord, I went back out into the kitchen. Sherry asked me if I was okay, and I said, "Yes, I would be fine, but let's go for a ride."

I did not look at Lori. I needed some separation right then, and she knew it. I told Julie "Bye," and we left. We drove around for a while and talked about the new baby and our children and their lives, just talking, and so I could wrap my head around the whole thing. Later, Sherry dropped me off, and I went into the house told Lori good night and went to bed. The next morning, I heard her throwing up in the bathroom, and then I understood why her sinus were so bad and making her sick in the mornings. It was not sinus but morning sickness. She got ready to go to work, and I kissed Wesley bye; he was going to daycare, and I kissed her bye too and told her to have a good day.

I got really excited about this new baby. Lori went to the doctor and found out we were getting another boy. Yes, I was ready for the new baby boy; she was going to name Carl Nathaniel Barrs. We are going to call him Nathan. We got things ready for the baby got a crib had a baby shower, and we were ready. We were just waiting on him, and it seemed he was taking his time; finally, he decided he was ready. I called Sherry and asked her to come and stay with Wesley while I drove Lori to the hospital. One of her friends stopped her on her street, and we did not think she was coming. I called her again, and she came right then. I got Lori in the car, and we were on our way when she said, "Mama, I can hardly sit down." I told her we are almost there; she held on, and I drove up to the valet service, and I jumped out of the car, calling for someone to get me a wheelchair please the baby was coming. A nurse ran to get a chair and told me she would take her up while I gave the guy my name and the keys to my car. The nurse that was helping told everyone to move; the baby was coming, and he did nine minutes after we got there; she was holding Nathan. He was beautiful, dark black hair, and bluish-brown eyes. I so wanted his eyes to be brown. I wanted a brown-eyed baby.

Well, I got one this time; his eyes are dark brown; they are beautiful just like him. I am so in love with this little fellow; my heart just swells with love for him. It's amazing how our hearts expand with love for each new baby.

He grew so fast and was a big healthy boy, but just like his brother, he, too, had ear problems. He was very young when they put tubes in his ears; other than that, he was fine. He looks just like Carl; he is so precious. Even though Lori was his mom, I loved taking care of him; he makes me smile—what a cute, funny personality he has. He is so happy to see you when you come into a room where he is. Another child of my heart; now I have three, and I love them all.

I was living my life trying to do the things that GOD wanted me to do. I taught children's church. I would look up stories in the Bible and find work sheets about the stories to help the children learn in a way it would stay with them. We read the stories first from the Bible then they did crosswords, fill in the blank, and coloring sheets. I was trying to get them to understand the moral of each story they had heard, and it seemed to work. I also fed them cookies and something to drink when they were done. I enjoyed this, and they seem to enjoy it too.

Carolyn and Ed came to my house most Sunday mornings so I could do her hair for her. I got up early so I could get me ready and Wesley and Nathan if they were at my house. Then we picked up Chelsea on our way if she was at her mother's house. We would have a full day, and if I could, I would take the grands out to eat afterward if their parents did not have plans.

I started another ministry at the church. We had a funeral dinner for one of the families, and the church asked everyone to please bring or drop off a covered dish. Well, I was afraid there would not be enough food to feed all the guest that came back to the church. I went out and picked up extra food so we would have enough food. I then approached Dr. Lindsay about me fixing the food for the funerals, and the people of the church donating to a funeral fund, so many of them had to go to work and did not have time to stop by with a covered dish. While I was there, it worked out well.

As I said earlier, I am a seamstress and enjoy sewing. I made some costumes for the church and I made Dr. Lindsay a robe that sheds water to wear when he is baptizing people, then I made white gowns for the people to wear while being baptized. Anything that they needed me to do, I tried to do. I was just trying to do what the LORD wants for his church. HE gave me the gifts I used to do the things I did. I do not take the credit; if not for HIM, I would not have been there.

My friend Sherry went to church with me on Wednesdays, and they welcomed her in too. She felt at home there but went to church with her husband on the weekends. Her husband, Dannie, worked the second shift, so she came over to my house in the afternoon. We did lots of things together. We went out to eat, swam in my pool, and we played Scrabble all the time. We were addicted to the game.

One evening, I got a call from Carolyn, and she told me she did not have enough money to get her heart medicine. I told her to tell Ed to go to the pharmacy and get the meds and to write a check. We would get some money before morning. When I hung up, I was praying about it when the phone rang again; it was Sherry. She said, "Let's go to Taco Bell." I told her I could not go; it was the end of the month, and I was waiting for payday on the third of next month. I maybe had $5 in the bank. She told me that was okay; she had a $20, and we could eat on that. I got ready, and she came to pick me up. When I went outside and got in the car, she said, "Okay, let's go."

I told her no, not yet. We needed to pray, and she said, "What's wrong?" I told her about my conversation with Carolyn, and she gasped. She said, "You don't have any money for her, do you?"

I told her no, but we were going to pray about that and GOD would fix it. So we prayed. I told GOD what I had done and that I could not fix this problem so I was giving it to HIM because I knew HE would find it for me. Then in a totally different state of mind, we went to Taco Bell. When we got there, we got our food and sat down to eat, but first, we prayed for or food and for Carolyn. While we were praying, my phone started ringing, and when we finished praying, I answered my phone. The call was from my nephew Bobby; he lived in Kansas. When I said hello, he said, "Aunt Betty, how are you?"

I said, "I'm fine. How are you?"

He said he and his family were fine. He then said, "I want to send you something, but I need to know how you want me to send it."

I told him he would have to tell me what it was for me to tell him. He told me it was the $400 dollars that he owed me. I was like, "What?"

He said, "You lent me some money and I want to pay it back."

I told him I had forgotten about it. He then said, "Do you want me to mail it or send it Western Union?"

I told him to please send it via Western Union to the Publix in town, so I could pick it up the next morning. He told me he would and said goodbye.

I looked at Sherry and could hardly breathe. GOD had answered our prayers like we could never have imagined. I knew HE would but not like that; all it takes is to put it in HIS hands and be patient and believe with unfailing faith. We ate our tacos and went back to my house so excited and praising GOD.

The next morning, I called Carolyn at 7:45 a.m. and told her to have Ed meet me at the Publix around 8:00 a.m., and I would give him the money to put it in the bank. I got ready and went to the store, and I was telling the lady behind the counter what a wonderful thing GOD had done. She was getting my money for me; she was amazed at my story and when she handed over the money she told me. See, GOD gave you the money for your friend and then blessed you with $300 extra dollars. She was right. I had not thought of that. GOD is so good, and you can't outgive GOD. I was walking on clouds of love and joy for my heavenly FATHER as I went out of the store.

Life goes on, and we all adjust to what is going on around us whether people are in our lives or not, that is something you learn as time goes by; you never forget them you just keep them in your heart.

I went to Michigan with Carolyn and Ed and Bonnie called me and told me that Cleo and his girlfriend Nikki got married. I was very surprised and a little hurt that he would do that when I was not around to help and celebrate with him and Nikki. I hoped this was going to be good for Cleo, Nikki, Krissy, Nikki's daughter, and my granddaughter Chelsea. Chelsea's life had been so disrupted for a couple of years. After her parents separated, she and her daddy lived with me, along with Lori and her boys. With a brief exception, when Cleo was with someone else, and her mother had married someone else to. None of these relationships lasted for any of them, which just made Chelsea's life chaotic; she spent days with us, days with her mom, and now she was going to live with Cleo and Nikki and Krissy. I was not sure all this would be good for her; since she was two years old, her life had been unsettled. I had great hopes, though; Nikki seemed to treat Krissy very well, so I hoped she would be good for Chelsea. Only time would tell.

I tried to insert my life into theirs in a small way; when Krissy had something going on at school, I tried to attend. I wanted her to feel like she was part of our family too, and I could be her mama just like I was Chelsea's. They started coming to church, which I though was a good thing for them all. My prayer was for all my children and grandchildren to be happy, fulfilled, and living for Christ Jesus.

We still did Christmas with Carl's parents just like we had done for the twenty-eight years that Carl was alive, and we continued doing that. Carl's daddy enjoyed seeing the grandchildren, and they all loved going to Grandmama's and Grandpa's. It was nice to see everyone doing so well and being with cousins and aunts and uncles. It was a good thing to teach the children they needed to learn to value family and to keep the people you love close at hand.

Chapter 15

Life was moving along smoothly I had made peace with the Lord where my son Jeremy was concerned. I felt sure that if something happened and I did not get to meet him on this earth, I would meet him in heaven someday. I told the Lord I would do whatever he wanted me to do with my life, and I was ready to go home when he called me.

Much to my surprise, that is not the kind of call I got. On February 14, 2008, I was at home alone and my phone rang and the ID on the phone said it was Roger M. Hilton. I answered the phone, and I knew something was wrong; why else would he call me? I had not talked to him since 1989 after Hurricane Hugo.

I said, "Hello," and he asked, "Betty?" I said, "Yes, this is Betty."

He wanted to know how I was doing, and I told him I was fine. He then proceeded to tell me that his wife Irene had passed away the month before and that his mother was very, very ill and in a nursing home in Summerville. I told him how sorry I was that his wife had passed away, and that I knew just how he felt. I also told him I would be praying for his mother, that she would recover. I asked him if there was anything I could do like sit with his mother or anything else; he told me no, that his sisters-in-law had everything in hand. We talked for a little while, and he asked about my children and grandchildren; I told him they were all okay.

He said he was coming down in a week or so to see his mom. I told him to call me, and we would have coffee. I understood what being alone was like and wanted to help if I could. The next time I heard from him, it was when he told me he had been here and gone back home, that his mother had a stroke and passed away too. I was heart sick for him. He also told me he had been awfully sick with a respiratory illness because he now had asthma. That he did not call me while he was here; he was the executor of his mother's will and had been busy. I told him that was fine; I understood. I had been there too.

We talked about Jeremy briefly, wondering to each other where he was and what he was doing. We worried about the fact that the Desert Storm war had taken place and we did not know where he was, and if he had been in the military, and if he was still alive. We both had the same thoughts about our child, and it was hard for us both to put it into words.

After that, I expressed my condolences again for the loss of his mother and told him I would talk to him again soon just to see how he was; he said that would be nice, and we both said goodbye. That was in late February, and I returned his call on Easter Sunday. I told him I knew what it was like being alone and hoped he was okay. He said he was fine and had started back to work. He had been out a year taking care of Irene. I really felt sorry for him; he was alone, and I had my children and grandchildren around me, which made my life totally different.

I called him at Easter just to check on him. I was by myself in the afternoon and thought he is having a hard time on holidays. I know he is because I did too. He told me he was doing all right, and I knew he would say that, but when you have been, there you can tell in other peoples' voices, and I recognized that sound.

I made a promise to myself to call him on the Fourth of July, and I did; it was better. He told me he had gone kayaking with his stepdaughter and a friend of hers, and he sounded in good spirits. I was so glad he was getting out and doing things. I did not call him on Halloween, which is my least favorite holiday, and if there were not grandchildren, I would not bother. I like sewing the cute costumes for them, but not what it represents to the world at large. However, I did dress Wesley up one time as Moses and Nathan had a frog costume to wear; he was a plague, the cutest plague you ever saw.

I did not talk to him again until Thanksgiving; he was home, doing okay, so he said. Slowly, he began to tell me about Irene, his deceased wife and how sick she had been. I just let him talk, and I interjected to make it easier; he needed that too. We also talked about his mom and what had happened to her and the stroke she had. It was sad, but it was good for him to talk about it to someone. I know he did not want to talk to Irene's family about her sickness. I think he would have been upset if he knew why I called him, and really, I liked hearing his voice. I always had and always would. I waited a long time and did not call him, not because of anything he did, but for myself, I wanted to protect him from the hurt and I knew I was falling back in love all over again. I had always loved this man, and I always would; he was a part of me that had been missing a long time, and I knew I would only get hurt, so I told no one that I talked to him or that I had called him. It was nobody's business but ours.

In September, Roger called me. I was really glad to hear his voice; he sounded better and more upbeat, if you will. He asked me how I was doing, and I told him I was great. I listened to him talk, taking in what he was saying and the sound of his voice. After chatting a while, he said, "I want to ask you a question."

I told him to go ahead. I was listening. He asked, "What do you think about us looking for Jeremy again?" I was surprised and elated. What if we could find him? I said, "Roger, I have to be completely truthful with you. I would love to look for Jeremy, but I don't have the money to do that. I live on social security."

He said, "That's not a problem. I can take care of that."

I said, "If we run into anything that requires money, you can take care of that? I will go to the reunion sites I contacted before and update all our information and do all the leg work here in Charleston."

He said, "That's great. When will we start?"

I said, "I will start right away to update everything. I need your address and other pertinent information, so let me get a pencil and paper to write it all down."

He gave me all the information I needed, and we talked a while and then he had to get ready to go to work; he was as excited as I was. When I told him bye, he said, "I'll call you tomorrow, bye."

I would have jumped up and down if I could jump up and down. I went to get the book and file I kept with all the information about Jeremy that I had and a record of the reunion sites I signed up on. It was not a lot. I had a printout from the hospital with his birth record, time, date, weight, and attending physician. The other information I had was the information my mother had given me that she found in the phonebook, written in her handwriting. I just stared at it she had such high hopes for me. As I read it, my heart mourned for her. I remembered the day we came home from the hospital without him; we both cried with broken hearts. I have to say after that my mother became my best friend. After what I put her through, I always tried to put her and her needs first before my husband and children. She was getting on in years and needed help; every time she got sick or had to have surgery, I packed up my children and went to stay with her. Carl did not mind; he went to see his parents a couple of times a week. Okay, enough reminiscing. Back to Jeremy and the search.

I contacted some search angels to help us look all over the country, and they did just that. Roger and I had an agreement. I would receive the information from the search angels and then forward it to him, and he would contact whoever it was. I was not comfortable calling some man I did not know, and then if I got his wife, what would I say? It was better all around if Roger did that part.

Roger ended up calling a doctor who was not adopted, a police captain who was sure he was not adopted, and several other Jeremy Andersons; they were not adopted, but they all wished him well in his search.

Just before Christmas, we had one that we thought was promising and were trying to decide what to do if this was him would I go to Maine or would he come to Charleston? He had a job and needed to be there at LL Bean at Christmas, one of their busiest times of the year. I told him I could not come there. I had thought about it and decided while I was teaching children's church. It would not be appropriate for me to come to his house, which is not the kind of example I was setting for my class.

He made the phone call to the Jeremy Anderson we had a number for, and I waited at home for him to call me back to let me know if it was him. When the phone rang, my heart was in my throat.

I answered with such hope, but again we were disappointed. The young man was not our son. I started to cry, and Roger told me it would be okay and that he had thought about it, and he had decided to come to Charleston at the end of January. Then we would talk to the attorneys he had hired and get as much information as possible.

Roger had been doing some work on this too, he called the South Carolina clerk of the Supreme Court and explained to them what we were doing and told them who our attorney had been in 1968 whom we assumed had passed away. The lady at the courts looked it up and said, "Yes, he had died and that his records had been turned over to another attorney for ten years." She then explained that the ten years were up, and the attorney that had the records had petitioned the court for permission to destroy them, so we had better hurry before the permission had been granted. She gave Roger the name and number of the attorney that was holding the records. He then called that attorney's office and spoke to the law assistant, and she told him those records are in storage and were inaccessible.

When he told me that I went up in flames, I said, "She does not want to look for them. Call them back and tell her I will look for them, just tell me where they are."

Roger said, "Hold on, they won't let you look for them, but I will call our attorneys and give them this information. Maybe they can get them to search for them."

I replied, "Okay, but we need those records."

We talked on the phone every day. I was walking in the mornings, and he was too, so sometimes, we walk and talked to each other. On January 1, 2010, New Year's Day, Roger had to work so while he was working. I updated the reunion sites I had originally joined back in 1989. Then I went looking for more and found some good ones. I put both our information onto them and looked to see if anyone had searched them for us. No such luck, I could not figure out who had come to Mama's house and where the information came from unless the birth parents had my name. I could not go to the courthouse again and check the books; after the hurricane, they had been transferred to microfiche, and I did not know where to begin. I had just gotten my own computer a couple of years before, so I was clueless.

Lori was teaching me as much as she could, and if I wanted to learn something, I usually asked the computer how to do it.

Roger made his plans to come to Charleston on Monday, January 25, so we could search and to return on to Maine on Monday, January 31. When he landed in Charleston, he called me and told me he would call me again when he got to his hotel. I was sitting at the table in my kitchen with Bonnie and Evelyn. They had come over for moral support. I had a different person cut my hair that day, and she had just about scalped me; all I wanted to do was cry. They told me it was fine, and I looked wonderful; they were just telling me that, but I love them anyway.

Cleo had been redoing my bathroom and had not finished; he drove up while I was waiting for Roger's phone call. He came to work on the bathroom. I told him, "Nope, you cannot do that. I have plans for the whole week, and I could not have my bathroom not working. It would have to wait." He said okay, and I told him that Jeremy's daddy was coming to town, and I was going to meet him shortly, so we could figure out what we were going to do first. He told me good luck and "I will see you later."

Shortly after he left, Roger called and told me he was at the hotel to come on over. It was like a six-minute drive from my house to the hotel. When I got there, I had to take a deep breath/ I was nervous. I had not seen him since 1989 and now it was 2010. I knew I had been through a lot in the last twenty years and four months and so had he. I was older and so was he; how would it be? The only thing I could do was walk into the hotel and find out. The doors opened with a whoosh, and I looked to the desk and then to the right and there he was, smiling that smile I always loved. We hugged each other and then he said, "Let's go sit over there so we can talk." Over there was a nice sitting area with a fireplace; it was convenient and out of the way. When we sat down, I said, "Have you eaten?" And he said no, so I told him, "Let's walk across the street and get something to eat."

We went across the street, thinking we would go to the deli and found it closed so we went to Zaxby's Chicken, and I ordered a salad, and he got a sandwich. We talked about general things while we ate.

I asked how his flight was, and he said fine. How much snow did he leave in Maine, things like that, he wanted to know how all my family was. I told him Bonnie and Evelyn came and had coffee with me earlier when they got off work.

We went back across the street after we had eaten and went right back to the place we had been sitting at the fireplace. It was nice and cozy and warm. I will never forget the first question he asked me, not in this lifetime anyway. He said, "Where is your hair and why is it orange?"

Aha! Now I knew how bad it looked. All I could do was laugh. He said, "Sorry, I did not mean to say that." The look on his face was so cute; he was real sorry. I told him, "That's all right. I had it cut today and my regular hairdresser was not there, so I let someone else cut it and it is too short, and as for the orange, I was trying for a natural color from when I was younger."

He said, "Oh."

After that, the ice was well and truly broken, and we began to talk about our lives just like we did when we were on the phone when we talked every day. It was so nice to sit and look at him; he was older, but so was I. I wondered if he thought I looked old and unattractive because he sure did not. I saw him just the way I always had, with love. We talked for a while about random stuff like where were we going to start in the morning and what time; we settled on 9:00 a.m. I told him, "I am going home, you get some rest, and I will see you in the morning." I got up and he held my coat for me; it felt so nice no one had done that in a long time, and the he walked me to my car, hugged me good night, and off I went.

I went home and got ready for bed, but first checking my computer to see if anyone was looking for information about our high school reunion we were having Memorial Day weekend. There were none, so I said my prayers and got into bed. Who was I kidding? I was not going to be able to sleep for a while and I knew that. I went back over everything that had happened and told myself to get some hair color and recolor my hair. Laughing at the way he looked when he said that out loud.

IN GOD'S TIME

The next morning, he arrived in a blue convertible he had rented at the airport; he was enjoying the weather in the south, wearing just long-sleeved shirt and a vest, and I was wearing a coat. I loved that smile on his face when he wheeled into my driveway. He had told me he had a red Corvette and from the look on his face now, I knew he loved driving it.

He asked me if I wanted to drive the convertible and I told him no; that was okay. He should drive. I knew he wanted to. We went to the high schools in West Ashley and asked to see the old yearbooks; that we were alumni parents and they let us look at them. We were searching for Jeremy Anderson and redheaded boys; we were under the impression that our son was a redhead just like the two of us. We looked a long time and under each year, hoping to see the son we were looking for we did this Monday, Tuesday, and Wednesday. We found no one with that name and no one that looked like we thought he should. After searching for hours and hours, we would have lunch and then ride around Charleston and the beaches, talking about the times we had been to these places years ago.

On Thursday, we went to the Charleston County Courthouse to check the records there. Roger knew all about microfiche and how to read them and operate the machines. I felt like this would work, and we would find something. We found lots of records and wrote down a lot of names and probably the same names I had written down years ago. I had not pulled that record book out. I would remember to get it out sooner or later. But for all our hard work, we really found nothing but people's names and the adoptions that our attorney had done back in 1968.

We were really tired and needed to eat, and Roger had sat at that machine. I could tell his back was bothering him; it was the way he moved when he got up to help me look for something else. He told me he had a bad back he had hurt when he was in the navy.

I have not said before, but he spent thirty years in the navy, serving our country from Vietnam to Desert Storm. He has paid his dues, and you would think being in the navy meant being on a ship, right? Well, he was not on a ship; he was in the air. He was a crew member on a plane; he did electronic intelligence and other jobs.

I was amazed when he told me the navy has more planes than the air force, and the army has more boats than the navy. I had no clue about the military and what went on. Three of my brothers went to Vietnam; one of them went twice and the one that went twice went to Korea when my other brother was there. The one that went to Vietnam twice was Will, my oldest brother. He was career army, and he went to Korea too. He went to Korea first with Kline, my second oldest brother, and then he went to Vietnam when Bob my third brother was there and then again when Ken my youngest brother went. Ken got married not long before he went. He is three years and two months older than me. Roger and I doubled with him and his wife.

Chapter 16

Thursday, January 28, was the day we spent the whole day in the courthouse. We were tired and hungry. We got something to eat and were relaxing at our table when Bonnie called me and asked how our search was going. I explained what we had been doing and having no luck, but we were hopeful for our appointment with the attorney in the morning. She asked us to come to her house for dessert, that Evelyn and Otto were coming too. I asked Roger, and he said okay, that was fine with him. We went back to Goose Creek to my house first and then to Bonnie and Karl's; they lived about two miles from me. We had a fun evening talking about the past and on a serious note about our search. They were all praying we would get the information we needed. After spending a couple of hours together, we started to relax, and I felt like Roger would be able to rest that night and maybe so would I; we were so tired, and our search was not over yet. We had not discussed what we were going to do next if the attorneys were unable to get the information. We left Bonnie's and he took me home and went to his hotel but not before telling me he would pick me up at eight fifteen the next morning for our appointment at 9:00 a.m. downtown. We were going early because of traffic and finding a place to park; it could be difficult that time of the morning. I told him I would be ready to go when he got there for him to go get some rest, and he said, "You get some rest too."

I went into my house. Lori and the boys were there to spend the night. I was glad she was there. She was always around when I needed her; she and I were like my mom and me. I am so glad I was there for my mom when she needed me. If she called, I went whenever, wherever. I did not care and neither did my family. Carl and the kids loved her. And they expected me to go to her when she needed me and if one of them were sick. She was at my house unless it was flu or something like that. After I got in and settled, I cleaned up the kitchen where the boys had had snacks and then went and took a much-needed, long, relaxing bath. I put on my nightgown and robe and sat down at my computer to catch up with my day and what was going on with my friends on Facebook.

It was nice to touch base with old and new friends. I sat there a while, and it was 1:30 a.m. when I looked at the clock, and I told myself to hurry and check my email to see if any one I knew needed tickets to the class reunion. I was checking the names of the people the emails were from I noticed a name I did not recognize. I left that one and continued with the others. When I finished, I went back to the one I had left and studied the name and was sure I did not know this person. I open the email not knowing what to expect and got the most amazing shock of my life. The email said, "YOUR SEARCH IS OVER I HAVE YOUR SON." Oh my goodness. I read it three times before I picked up my phone to call Roger. His cell phone rang and rang; he did not answer. What was I going to do? I could not call the hotel; he had just told me today there was something wrong with his room, and they had moved him. Now I don't know where he is, and I can't wait until tomorrow morning to tell him.

I was really freaking out, and Lori heard me and came to my room and asked what was wrong. I said, "Read that."

She did and replied, "Is that from Jeremy's mother?"

She said, "Why are you so upset? I understand why because of the message but what else is wrong?"

I told her with my voice getting louder and louder, "Roger won't answer his phone, and I can't call the hotel they moved him, and I don't know which room he is in."

She said, "Mama, sit down before you have a stroke or heart attack. I will take care of this." I forgot that she had been a hotel manager. She called the hotel and told them it was an emergency, and she needed to get in touch with Mr. Hilton and that she understood they had moved him to a new room to please connect her to his room. When the phone started ringing, she handed the phone to me. It rang several times and then Roger's groggy voice answered with a

"Hello." I hurried and said, "Roger, you have to come over here right now. I have an email from what looks like Jeremy's mother. Come help me figure this out."

Roger responded with "Betty?"

I said, "Yes, this is Betty. Did you hear what I said?"

He replied, "Something about an email and Jeremy's mother."

I said, "Yes, I have an email that says she is his mother. You need to come over here and read this."

"Now?" he asked.

"Yes, now," I replied.

His next response was "Okay, I'll be there shortly." And he hung up the phone. Lori was watching me and said, "Well?"

That's when I realized I was in my nightgown and robe. I could not meet him at the door dressed like this. I put on the first things I could find a pair of jeans and an old soft top I liked to wear, but first I needed underclothes. I got it all together and got dressed and put on my slippers. I never walk around barefooted. I am a diabetic, and I constantly worry about my feet. One of my daddy's brothers lost his leg up to his knee and that was not going to happen to me.

It was not long, and I saw the lights of the car pull into my driveway I was watching for him. I opened the door as soon as he reached the porch. I did not want him to ring the doorbell the others were asleep. He came in and I said, "The computer is in my bedroom come read this email and tell me if it is real!"

He sat down at the computer and read the email, then he read it again. "When did you find this?" he asked.

I said, "About thirty minutes ago. I tried to call you, but you did not answer your phone."

He looked at me with sleepy eyes and smiled and said, "I was asleep."

"Duh, like I figured that out. Or you just did not want to talk in the middle of the night," I replied.

"So what are we going to say to this lady?" I asked him.

He sat down at the computer and read what she had put in the email, first her statement about having our son, how much Jeremy weighed at birth, how long he was and who the attending physician was. This was information only she would have. He started doing something else on the computer, so I asked him, "What are you doing?"

He answered me while he typed, "I am checking the other webpage we set up, the Jeremy search site, to see if she put any information there."

Then he stopped talking when he got to what she had entered to that page. "She has the attorney's name right and the hospital," he said. He started typing and reading what he was typing aloud to me. This is what he typed, "We are amazed and elated at your email. Please contact us as soon as possible at 843-303-1720." He hit send and stood up. I could not help myself I hugged him, and I said, "You need to go and get back to sleep. Sorry I woke you, but I could not wait till morning to tell you."

He replied, "No, that is fine. I'm glad you did. I never imagined we would get an email like that."

I said, "I didn't either. I almost freaked out. I think I read it a few times before I reacted. That's when I started calling you, and when you did not answer, I was making noises and Lori came to see what was wrong. When I showed her what the email said and I told her I was trying to call you, she told me to sit down before I had a stroke or heart attack then she took over calling the hotel and finding out which room you were in and having them ring your room. She used to be the manager of a hotel in North Charleston. She knew what she was doing. Thank goodness for Lori. I did not want to drive over there to tell you what was in that email. I can hardly believe it now. We will have information for the attorneys in the morning. Maybe his mother will call us in the morning. You go get some rest. I'll be ready in the morning."

I walked with him to the front door, and he hugged me bye. He replied over his shoulder, "You go to bed and get some rest too. Good night." After he drove out of the driveway, I turned to go to bed, wondering if his insides were shaking as much as mine. How extraordinary this evening had been. God was in control, I could see that, and I was so thankful. As I turned the lights off and was getting ready to say my prayers before going to sleep, I wondered when God started all this. I could see HIM working in my life. When I got to my knees to pray, all I could say to my LORD was "Thank you" and "YOU are wonderful." Words were beyond me. I said my regular prayers and crawled off the floor and into bed, and I did go to sleep.

The next morning, January 29, 2010, I got up with Lori to get the boys ready for school and started getting myself ready for the day. I knew it was going to be busy. Roger came right on time, and I was ready to go. I had already had coffee and breakfast, so I was in go mode. When he started getting out of the car, I went outside and said, "Good morning, do you need to come inside?"

He replied, "Good morning, and no if you are ready, we will leave now." I walked to the car and got in; he did likewise. I said, "Did you get any more sleep after you got back to bed?"

He said, "Actually I did, I guess I was tired, and you?"

I told him, "Yes, I did. I was tired too and felt sure everything was going to be all right, that email just blew me away, what a wonderful, caring, and compassionate woman, the mother of our son must be. It is like adoptions are today the child grows up knowing their birth mother and sometimes the father too. But I'm not sure we would have managed that under the circumstances."

Roger said, "You are probably right."

I told him, "Bonnie asked me if she could adopt our baby and I had to tell her no. I was sure I could not be around him and not want to be his mother. I have a hard enough time when around other people especially when they discipline their children. It would not have worked, and I was sure I could not be around when it was my child." I then told him how I use to deal with customers that came into the bookstore.

I said, "I used to have a lot of sailors that came into the store with their wives and children, and the dads I know had Napoleon complexes, the children would be children and the dads would growl at the children, and before they could start in on the children for being children, I would go around the counter and get the children and take them to the children's books. I told them to pick out one they would like to read, and we would read them together. I felt sure they had a good time and was not punished for being children. I can tell you if he, the father, had hit one of those children I probably would have gone to jail for hitting him, or I would have called the police. So no, having a relationship with our son while he was growing up with other parents would not have been an option for me. I carry to much baggage to live through that. I did all the discipline in our house when Cleo and Lori were growing up because Carl knew I would freak out if he started spanking them with a belt. The reason I know this is because I was standing in the kitchen with my mom at her house one day, and Cleo came running in the house and stood behind me in the corner of the cabinets. I could feel him shaking, and before I could ask him what was wrong, his dad came in the house, and as he cleared the front door, he pulled his big belt out of his jeans and folded it in half and as he did I pressed Cleo further back into the corner and got in front of him."

Carl said, "Betty, move, I am going to give him a spanking." I unfortunately was not so inclined.

I told him, "Over my dead body, and you have to understand I was almost eight months pregnant with Lori."

He just looked at me, but I was not through with him yet, poor guy. I said, "After the life my mother has lived with my father, how dare you come into her house and act like that." He apologized to my mother and turned to go outside and over his shoulder he said, "Cleo ran out into the road in front of a car and scared me to death."

I told him, "I will deal with it," and I did. Cleo had to sit inside and not go back out to play. I know my children did not know why their father did not often get after them but that was why. When Cleo and Chelsea came to live with me, Lori, and Wesley, I reacted the same way when Cleo would get after her. I can't help it I try to control it, but I can't I even talk to children in the stores when I'm shopping when they are about to get in trouble with their fathers. It's just men. I don't think I like them very much, and I certainly cannot watch a TV show or read books where there is child abuse. I get mad at every man I see and talk too." By the time I finished telling Roger how I felt and why I knew I could not have had an open adoption, we were almost at the lawyer's office.

He parked the car, and we got out and were walking to the office when I realized he had not said much while I was telling him my story. So I asked him, "Could you have lived with knowing the people who adopted Jeremy, having another dad and mom raise him while you watched?" He replied no. "And I was not to worry Jeremy was a grown man now, almost forty-two years old." We went into the office with hopes that they had gotten the records from the other attorney or they and had gotten the information we needed to find our son. We were disappointed when Mr. Overton told us that no; they had not been able to get the file, but they had not given up either, and they did not have the information we needed, and he had not been able to contact the office manager of our original attorney. I felt deflated when he got through telling us that while assuring us they would keep trying. When he had finished telling us all that, I told him about the email I had received the night before. I told him exactly what it said, and he asked me to please send it to him so he could make sure it was from Jeremy's mother. I said I would, and we got up to go thanking him for his time and again reassuring him I would send a copy of the email.

Roger and I were walking down Church Street going to the car when I asked him, "What are we going to do now? Where are we going?" He looked me straight in the eye and said, "We do not have Krispy Kreme in Maine, and I want some doughnuts." I laughed and he said, "I'm serious. Do you want some too?"

I told him, "Of course, I do. Who doesn't want doughnuts?" The smile he gave me was wonderful; he looked like he did all those years ago. That same handsome face and beautiful smile I fell in love with forty-four years ago. I felt like a teenager for a few minutes, the same quickening of my heartbeat and the catch in my breath. I know we are now old, but sometimes it catches you off guard and you feel young again. It was a wonderful feeling. I was basking in the sunshine of a winter day, enjoying our leisurely walk to the car we were not in a hurry we had time, but inside we were waiting for my phone to please ring. We got in the car, and I reminded him where the Krispy Kreme was and he said, "The same place?"

And I told him, "Yes, the same place." We drove over the bridge to West Ashley talking about what kind of doughnuts we liked best. He liked lemon, and I knew that he also likes lemon meringue pie, which is my favorite too. It's amazing the things we have in common we have found out a lot about each other since we started talking on the phone most mornings. That, too, made it like old times.

We got to Krispy Kreme quickly; traffic was light by then, and most people were at work. We went in and ordered the kind of doughnuts we wanted and coffee. We were watching the people around us and eating our yummy doughnuts and not talking much, our morning started early, and we were taking a breather. Then, my phone rang. It was in his vest pocket. I had handed it to him so I would not have to carry a purse. We both froze, and then I said, "Hand me my phone. It might be that lady." He reached into his vest pocket with what seemed like slow motion to me, and finally, I had my phone. I jumped out of my chair and turned my back to the room so I could hear when I answered. I said, "Hello?" There was a pause and then a gentleman said, "May I speak to Betty Bounds Barrs?"

I replied, "This is she."

Then he said, "This is Richard Jeremy Bearden—"

And I cut in and said to him, "Jeremy, I know who you are, son. I am in a restaurant with your birth father. Please hold on while we go to the car, so we can talk to you with the speaker of my phone on."

He said, "Yes, ma'am."

After I said that, I turned around and screamed at Roger and everyone in the room, "It's him, it's him, come on, Roger, we have to go outside to the car and talk to him."

Everyone in the restaurant were looking at us, and they knew it was him, but not who he was. We walked out and got in the car, and I said, "Jeremy, are you there?"

And he said, "Yes, ma'am."

I wanted to hug him just from the sound of his voice. Then I said, "Jeremy, Roger is here, and he wants to talk too."

When Roger said, "Hello, Jeremy," Jeremy replied, "Hello, sir," and my estimate of our son continued to rise. What a nice young man. We talked to him for an hour or more, we asked him how he was, and he told us he was fine. Then right up front we told him why we had given him up for adoption, that we were sixteen and eighteen when he was born, and we knew we could not give him the things we wanted for him. He told us, "You did the right thing. I have had a wonderful life." Then he told us he was glad to hear our side of the story his mother had been told that we were in college and did not want a child. I could have cried because that was so not true. I told him no that was wrong. We had loved him his whole life and had worried about him too.

Roger and I looked at each other, and we began to silently weep. Nobody else on this Earth knew what we were feeling. As much as people love us, they have no idea of the worry and loss and the mourning we have endured for the last forty-two years. To be talking to him like this was a gift from GOD, and we knew we were blessed. I then asked him if he had ever looked for me, and he said, "No, ma'am, why?" I told him about the two visits my mom had from someone. "Whose name was Jeremy, and she thought your last name was Anderson." He then asked, "When was that?"

I told him, "In 1986 and again in 1989."

I also told him it was before she got Alzheimer's disease. She did not tell me the first time, but she told my oldest sister, and there was nothing wrong with her then. She lived alone so she did not open the door because she was scared, so she talked to him through the door. He said again, "No, ma'am. I was in high school in Connecticut in 1986, and in 1989, I was in the navy stationed in Hawaii."

We asked him if he had any health problems, and he told us no that he was fine. I asked about high blood pressure because we have both had it since we were in our twenties, and he answered, "No, ma'am." Then he said, "You would not know it to look at me, but I have terrible eyesight" and we said at the same time, "We're sorry because we do too."

Then he told us he had to have his gallbladder removed and again we said we're sorry because we both did too. He asked Roger what he did, and Roger told him he had been in the US Navy for thirty years and he now lived in Maine where he had retired and then went to work for LL Bean as a systems analyst. He told Roger that he had been in the US Navy too, that when he went in; he wanted to be on a submarine like his dad but he had ended up in naval intelligence. Roger did laugh then because that was what he had done all those years while flying with an aircrew. I thought to myself, *Well, that apple did not fall far from the tree.* He told us he was married and had two little girls; the oldest was named Ana and the youngest was named Sophie. Roger and I both inhaled sharply, and we were stunned; that was Roger's mothers name. He told us Sara was his wife's name, and when he got home from work, he would make us his friend on Facebook. I told him not to rush and to talk it over with his wife that they had children to think of. He told us it would be fine we knew he was at work that he was a vice president of an engineering firm. He told us his parents had two other boys that were born after they adopted him. We were so pleased that he had siblings and was not an only child. We love our siblings and was glad he has two. We told him we were from big families that Roger had one sister and three brothers and I had two sisters and four brothers and that we were both next to the youngest in our families. So we talked a little longer, and then, before we hung up the phone, I told him, "Jeremy, we are not going to ever call you. If you want us in your life, you will have to call us. We just wanted to know you were alive and all right, son."

Roger gave him his phone number too. He said thank you sir to Roger, "I will talk to you later." After we heard him hang up the phone all we could do was hold each other and cry. This special gift God had given us was so precious, and we were so thankful. He was all right; he was healthy, happy, and he had a family and was doing fine. It was more than we expected, but we were so happy; we were giddy.

Chapter 17

Now we really had news for our families. I called Evelyn and told her we had just talked to Jeremy on the phone, and he lived in Knoxville, Tennessee. She was like, "What? Are you kidding me?"

And I said, "No, we are not. We really did talk to him for over an hour." Then I told her I had to go so I could call Bonnie.

She said, "No, wait. I have more questions."

I looked at Roger with a question in my eyes and said, "We could come to your house for coffee."

Roger nodded yes and she said, "Okay, come on."

I called Bonnie and told her what I had told Evelyn, and she was just as amazed. She, too, was full of questions I told her we would be over later to give her all the information. She was more restrained than Evelyn was. She said okay. I called Lori and told her because she knew what we found out last night and would be so glad for us. I also called Cleo and told him, but I figured Bonnie told Nikki and maybe she had told Cleo. I called the rest of my family, and Roger called his too; they were all amazed and so happy for us. All I needed to do was get on my knees and thank the Lord for this wonderful gift. When I finally got home later in the evening, I did just that.

I invited Evelyn and Otto over to have dinner with Roger and me on Saturday night, so that afternoon, I was in the kitchen preparing dinner when Roger who was on my computer called me to my room and said, "Look, Jeremy's mother put up pictures of Jeremy and his family." I was enthralled, but when he got to the pictures, she put up of Jeremy when he was a newborn, I had to leave the room. I started crying so hard I was making an awful racket.

I was trying to catch my breath when Roger came in to the kitchen and turned me around from the refrigerator where I was leaning and pulled me into his arms and held me while I cried. I could tell he was affected by the pictures because of the way his voice sounded. I later rather than sooner got myself back together and was able to finish dinner and talk to Roger about the pictures. Oh my goodness, he looks like us; he has my eyes and dimples and Roger's nose and chin. That nose is just like Roger's.

I told Roger, "You have a Roman (roaming) nose. It roams all over your face, and his does too. I am not surprised about how Jeremy looks. My mother told me he looks more like you than you other two children, and he looks like Roger too." I keep hearing the things she said about Jeremy in my mind. I never doubted someone visited her, but the more I thought about it and went over it in my mind, I finally had an epiphany; she thought she heard Jeremy Anderson and what was said was "And I am her son." If you say it fast, it sounds like *Anderson*. After a while, I knew in my heart that the LORD sent an angel that looked like Jeremy to my mother to give her some peace about her grandson and to get me started on this journey I am taking now with Roger. When you look at it from this perspective, it all fits, and I now believe we have no idea of the greatness of GOD and what he does.

I invited Roger to attend church with me on Sunday morning, and he said he would. I had already told Pastor Lindsay and his wife Debbie what had happened and asked if I could tell the church. Pastor agreed; it would be okay. So when he asked me to stand up with Roger and give them my news, I did just that. They needed to hear this news; they had prayed with me about this search and when GOD answers prayer, it is a confirmation of everything we believe in. Then we all did what came naturally; we praised our LORD for the answered prayer.

After church, we went to visit Roger's sister, Jean; she lives in Macedonia, South Carolina, about half an hour away. She was so excited to see us. Like the rest of the family members, she had questions and we had the answers. We tried to answer all the questions we knew the answers to, and that made her happy. When we left there, we went to visit Roger's niece that lives in Bonneau, South Carolina, a short distance from her Aunt Jean. She had heard the news from her parents who live in Texas. Roger had called them and gave them the news. Everybody in our families were so happy for us, and they were all thanking GOD for the gift we had received. We stayed there a short while, people that work and have children in school are always busy, and we needed to get back; we had to have an early dinner so Roger could get back to his hotel so he could fly back home in the morning early.

    We went to my house and had leftover chicken for dinner, then I told him good night, not goodbye because I was following him to the airport in the morning. We never stopped talking; we always had something to talk about, Jeremy, his children, those two beautiful little redheads, or you could say strawberry blondes. I was in love with them and I had not met them yet and was not sure I would get to because if only one of us gets to meet Jeremy. I am sending Roger. I have children and grandchildren. Jeremy is Roger's only child by birth, and I think he needs this, and I will make sure he gets it if possible. I guess you now know, yes, I am in love with him all over again. It was inevitable. All I had to do was hear his voice and see him again, but that was not necessary. I have always loved him and Jeremy. It did not take anything from Carl and my children whom I adore; my heart just had room for all of them, just like it does when I add new grandchildren. I added Nikki to my heart and her daughter Krissy when Cleo married them, and yes them; when a man marries a woman with a child, he should love the child too. That is what Roger did when he married his first wife, Irene; she had three children. Your heart just expands; the more love you give, the bigger your heart is. I'm not saying that everything is always perfect; we are all people with emotions and expectations, and we sometimes get things out of sorts, and people get their feeling hurt and lash out in the wrong way, but when you love them, you forgive them. The best example we have of that is JESUS. HE loved us when we were sinners, and loves us when we fall; if we all followed HIS example, the world would be a happier place.

    Roger said good night and told me what time to be ready to leave in the morning, and then he was gone. I was alone at my house; the children had gone back to their house. A new week was starting, and they had school tomorrow and Lori had to work, and her husband Henry was there with the animals. I got my clothes ready for the morning and took a long, much-needed soak in my tub. Afterward, I was real tired and ready for bed. I said my prayers and crawled into my bed. The next thing I knew, it was morning, and I got up and had coffee and breakfast and was ready to go.

Roger called me on his way over to my house, so I went to my car and started it up to warm it up; that way, I would be there and ready when he got there. He pulled in behind my car, and I opened my door to let him know I was ready. He smiled and said, "I will see you there." He backed out, and I did, too, right behind him, and we were off. I went to the parking garage at the airport, and he took his car to the rental place to turn his car in. I met him in the front of the ticketing counter he had to go to. He checked in and then we went to find us some coffee. We had about two hours before he was to leave. We talked about Jeremy, and if we would hear from him, we did not know for sure if he would call. We were praying he would, and somehow, I expected he would. I told Roger not to worry, just think of what we had already gotten in just one phone call, how blessed we were to have gotten that.

He agreed with me, and shortly, it was time for him to get in line for TSA precheck. I told him I would stay until he went beyond the barrier. We continued to chat, and I was dreading saying goodbye to him even though he promised to come back in May. He was going to drive his red Corvette down from Maine and take me to my high school reunion. He was at the entry part for TSA. I hugged him by and kissed his cheek, and he said, "I will call you when I get home."

I said, "Okay, be safe."

Then I turned and walked away, and I did not look back because I had tears running down my face and did not want him to see. I went to my car and drove straight to Bonnie's house so I could cry there; big sisters are wonderful.

Chapter 18

Roger called me when he got home and every day after that unless I was going out, taking my mother-in-law Hannah to breakfast and then shopping. When he called, I talked to him in the mornings until noon, and then he would take a nap before going to work at 2:00 p.m.; he worked until midnight. Then he would call me at his lunch time at 8:00 p.m., and again on his way home, we would talk till he was in the house and got into bed. We said good night and started over the next day.

We were wondering if Jeremy was going to call one of us; we talked about that and Roger felt sure he would call me first because I was his birthmother. I wanted him to call Roger first so he would know he wanted a relationship with him. That is exactly what Jeremy did; he called Roger and I was so happy for Roger. He deserved this; he is a good man, and he truly loves his son. I could hear it in his voice. They had so much to talk about; the fact that they were both in the navy and both in intelligence, it is wonderful for them and then Jeremy told Roger what his degree was in, and lo and behold, when Roger got out of the navy, he went back to school and got his second degree, which is the same as Jeremy's.

Jeremy called me too, and I was glad to hear from him. I think it was a little harder for us because all I could tell him about was his brother and sister and their families. I also told him about his aunts and uncles and that we had a very large family, and we were very close. Someone asked me if it bothered me that he called Roger first, and I said no, and I wasn't I was very glad it happened that way for them.

I went to Bonnie's one day to color her hair, and she colored mine while we were doing that. She asked me what was next, and I told her I was not sure except Roger was coming in May. He is taking me to my class reunion, and he was driving down in his red Corvette.

She said, "You know he really is in love with you."

I told her, "I don't think so. He does not come across that way to me."

She said, "I know for a fact he is just like he used to. I could see it while you were seated at the table the night before you found Jeremy."

I asked her, "What do you mean?"

So this was her response: "Both of you were sitting on the back side of the table the night we had coffee and dessert, and he could not keep his hands off of you. He was either patting your hand, holding it, or he had his arm around your shoulder, just as possessive as he always was. You wait and see if I'm not right, maybe he doesn't know it yet but he's already there," she said.

I told her, "I sure hoped she was right because I love him too.

She said, "I know how much you love him. Your face lights up when you talk about him, and when your phone rings and it is him, but you have loved him since you were fourteen years old." Bonnie more than anyone understood where I was coming from; she is married to her first love. When she was a senior in high school, our father broke up their relationship and would not let her see Karl anymore. They went their different ways, and he married someone else, and she did too. After being married to her first husband for thirty-four years, he wanted a divorce, and the night before she had to go to court, she met Karl again, and the rest is a wonderful story.

I talk to Evelyn about what Bonnie said, and her response was not what I expected. She told me in no uncertain terms, "He had better not hurt you again."

I told her, "I'm a grown woman now. I'm not sixteen anymore."

She replied, "You will always be fourteen years old where Roger Hilton is concerned."

I told her, "That does not take away how much I loved Carl."

She told me, "I know that. Carl and you had a very special relationship, and if he were still alive, you would still be married to him and loving him like you always did."

I replied, "Thank you very much."

I said, "Don't want anyone to imagine I did not love Carl because I did. My children know it, and I hope everyone else does too."

Life was moving slowly, but we were happy with the way things were going. Jeremy called us about every two weeks, and after he called us, we talked about our conversations with him. Every nugget of information about him and his family was like a piece of gold to us. We were trying to fill in the missing pieces we had lost; we realized that was impossible, but we shared what we knew. Having him back in our lives was like when you are starving for air underwater, and you break the surface, and you take a deep breath and air fills your lungs. You feel safe and renewed or maybe the word is complete—yes, complete. It fills you up. My heart swells with love for Jeremy, and I can share that with Roger because we both feel that way and always have felt like that.

Roger called me in the afternoon while he was at work. He had just talked to Jeremy and he had a question to ask me. I told him, "Okay, I am ready," but underneath, I was scared; maybe something was wrong, He said Jeremy called to ask him if he would come to Charleston a week early in May and then asked the two of us to come to North Carolina at his mother's house so we could meet him and his family. I was ecstatic. "Me too? What a wonderful surprise."

I said to Roger, "Will you be able to get off for that?"

His reply was, "Nothing will keep me from going nothing."

I concurred. Oh, for heaven's sake to see him, to touch him, I have waited forty-two years for this, and I know Roger had too.

So Roger said, "What do you think, can you go?"

I told Roger, "Nobody is going to stop me, GOD has sent us another miracle."

I asked Roger, "Did you ever imagine this would happen?"

He replied, "I was praying it would, and I know you were too."

I responded with "Not only was I praying but my family, your family, and my church, we were all praying for this. How wonderful our GOD is and Jeremy and his mother too."

That is what we talked about for days—Roger and me, that is. Roger had to go shopping because he needed clothes to wear in the south; in Maine, it was still cold. It did not get real warm there until the end of June. We planned his wardrobe for Charleston weather. He had clothes to wear to but not summer clothes, and in Charleston, in May, it is summer. I told him what the agenda was for the class reunion. Friday night meet and greet at the high school, Saturday, an all-day picnic with southern barbecue at the plantation at the Weapons Station, and a dance on Sunday night, with heavy hors d'oeuvres. It was going to be a full weekend. Adding to that the biggest day of our lives since we met, finally getting to meet Jeremy and his family. How can you even say that without an outburst of emotion?

When I told Bonnie, she and I both cried, what a blessing just to know him and talking to him on the phone but to meet him, hug him, I could hardly contain myself, just thinking about it. Bonnie wanted to know things like how long we would be with them, and what we were going to do? I told her that we were going to Cindy's house on Saturday morning, and after that, I had no clue; that was up to him.

Evelyn was just as excited as Bonnie she was so happy that both of us were going to meet Jeremy and family. I knew she was worried about that after I told her I would send Roger if only one of us could go meet him. She wanted to know what I was wearing, and I told her I was making some new outfits to wear, walking shorts and tops so I would not be hot. That I had things planned for the class reunion too.

I was talking Roger one morning when I got a call from Pastor Lindsay. I asked Roger to hold on and answered the other line. Pastor Lindsay asked if I was busy, and I told him no, I was just talking to Roger. His only comment was "I won't keep you. I just have some slacks I need you to hem please?"

I told him fine. "I will be here all day drop them by."

He replied, "See you later."

I went back to Roger and told him about the call; he knew I did things like that sometimes. We continued to talk this was a Monday;

he did not have to work he only worked four days a week but ten hours a day. We were still talking later in the when my doorbell rang. I went to answer it and there was Pastor Lindsay at the door. I said, "Hello."

He was laughing when he saw the phone to my ear; he said, "Are you still talking to that man, Roger?" teasing me.

I replied, "Yes, I am. Hand me the slacks and you talk to him." While I took the slacks to hang up, he stood on my porch and talked to Roger. I went back to the door, and he was teasing Roger about talking to me all day. They had met before, and it was all fun and games. He told Roger, "I will give you back to the lady. You have a good day," and to me he said, "Call me when the slacks are ready." He was gone, and I continued talking to Roger, which I loved to do; sometimes he even played his guitar and sang to me just like the old days.

Anyway, on Wednesday night, when I went to church, Pastor Lindsay asked me, "That guy you talk to all the time, has he told you he is interested in you?"

I told him, "No, we just talk, we have lots in common, and we are going to meet our son." Then he replied, "Let me clue you in. If a man talks to a woman on the phone that long, he is definitely interested."

I told him, "We will see."

May came around, and I was so happy. I went to Bonnie's for a cookout; it was nice. My children and grandchildren were there and other members of our big family; we had a wonderful time. I have a picture of Bonnie, Evelyn, and me in Bonnie's kitchen. Our children are all friends, and the grandchildren got along too. It makes for wonderful family gatherings. I have never figured out why brothers and sisters cannot get along. I was worried after Mama died that things would change, but she had taught us by example to love each other, and we did. If one of us needed something all they had to do was call one of the other six, if they could not help, they would find someone else who could help. With me being a widow, it was like having a warm blanket always wrapped around me. They all know nothing they could ever do or say would make a difference. I love them with my whole heart and always will.

I was finishing up getting my things ready for the trip to North Carolina. I did not have to get my hair done. I was letting it grow. I did not dare cut it and have Roger ask me where it went. I had also put it back to my regular color too. I think it is funny what he said, and he tells me in a stern voice, "That was not my finest moment." I will never forget it, though. I laugh when I think of it and the expression on his face after he said it.

Roger was on his way here, and guess what we talked on the phone for almost the whole trip, except when he had to stop and eat and get gas for the Corvette, and while he stopped for the night to rest and sleep. Then he was back in the car and on his way again; he called me so we could talk. I knew the route he was driving, and we discussed the traffic, the weather, and the crazy drivers. He has a condo rented at Short Stay outside of Moncks Corner; it is a military installation, and the prices are nice, and it is on the water too. He rented a two-bedroom so I could come and spend the night that way he would not have to come to my house to get me the next morning. When he got there, I left my house to go there; he was waiting so we could go get some dinner. It was wonderful to see him; it had been three and a half months. We had dinner and came back to the condo. To sit and talk just like we do on the phone. I showed him the things I got for the girls, and Jeremy and Sara. Friday, May 21, while we are traveling up, there is Sophie our youngest granddaughter's birthday; she will be six years old. Ana turned eight years old on the twenty-ninth of April, so I made funny things for them like flip-flops with bows and ribbon on them. We went to bed early; he needed to lie down and rest his back after driving all day. He has problems with his back and has for a long time. It is something that happened to him in the navy. I went to bed first so he would go take a shower and relax. I was going to read, which was my favorite pasttime. I set my phone alarm and read until I was sleepy.

My alarm woke me early, so I was up when I heard him stirring in his room. I waited for him to finish in the bathroom, and then I got ready to go. We only had a three-hour ride, but we were going to go easy and have fun doing it, and we were both anticipating what tomorrow was going to bring. He had booked two rooms at a hotel in Lenoir, North Carolina for us, and we could not check-in early so we stopped for breakfast then later for lunch, making our way ever closer. As we rode, we talked about our families and what they were thinking about our trip knowing they all wished us the best. We also talked about Jeremy and his family and what we thought our visit was going to be like. We had remarkably high hopes, and I prayed a lot.

    We checked in to our hotel, and I could tell Roger's back was bothering him, so I suggested he rest it a while, and he said after we have dinner. We went to dinner and came back, then I suggested that he lay across the foot of his bed, and I give him a back rub, and he was fine with that. I could feel the tightness of his back and knew it was hurting more than he said, so I really worked on it a long time so he would get some relief. We talked about what time we were leaving in the morning and how long it would take us to get to Cindy's home. I told him I needed to make a stop in the morning for a fruit basket for Cindy; in the south you do not go to someone's house especially the first time empty-handed. Shortly thereafter, I told Roger, "Good night," I was going to my room and get myself ready for tomorrow and asked if he needed anything ironed. He said, "No," and I asked, "What are you wearing?" Just like a mother, this man has lived all over the world, and I think I need to take care of him. He laughed and showed me what he planned to wear. I said, "The shirt needs ironing, give it to me." He was still laughing when he handed it over. I ironed his shirt and said good night. I know he thinks I am bossy, but I have been the caretaker of everyone in my life for a very long time.

Chapter 19

The day had finally come, May 22, 2010, the day we would meet our son. The fact that he is grown man and forty-two years old did not matter; he is our son, and we have always loved him. I heard Roger moving around in his room when I was getting ready. I guessed he was making coffee, so glad he was I need it to have it in the mornings to open my eyes, and I know he is the same. Soon, there was a knock on my door, and thankfully, I was ready. I knew he would be ready too. We needed to get started, and I had to stop to get a fruit basket. I called a store and talked with the produce people and asked if they could make me a fruit basket and they told me, "Yes, ma'am, be glad to. We have some made up."

I asked if any of them had pineapples in them, and he told me no they did not. I very nicely asked him if he would make me one with a pineapple; he said it will be extra. I told him that was okay. I just need a pineapple included. He said he would, and I thanked him. He told me to come to the produce department when I arrived. I had one more stop to make, and Roger was looking at his watch, very patiently, he asked, "Where else?"

I told him, "I need balloons for the girls for their birthdays."

Poor man, he just shook his head and drove to the dollar store; we got the b balloons and he said, "I'm following your lead on this. I have never had granddaughters before."

We picked up the fruit basket and started driving to our much-anticipated meeting. While we were driving, Roger's phone rang; it was Jeremy. Jeremy asked him if we had changed our minds about coming. Roger told him no. We were on our way there and would be there shortly. We were only a few minutes away and told him bye. We were pulling up into the driveway when this big, broad-shouldered, good-looking man came down the steps. Oh my goodness, my heart was pounding a million times a minute. He is so handsome, and he was smiling. He came around to my side of the car and opened my door and helped me out of the car, and as soon as I got out, I hugged him; it was a long time coming.

I said, "Hello, Jeremy," and he said hello too. Then I kissed him on the cheek; it was a dream come true, but I held it together and did not cry. After letting me hug him again, he went around the car to shake hands with Roger, and after he shook hands, they hugged each other, then I cried. I knew Roger's eyes were full, but he was doing his best to hold it together, and I am proud that we did so well. I knew later we would talk about this and cry to our hearts' content. Jeremy did not know it yet, but he just met the person that would stand beside him or behind him wherever he needed him while there is breath in Roger's body. His love for Jeremy is a love that is completely unmatched, and it goes without saying "I love all my children" like that. This gift we have from GOD has completely transformed our lives.

Jeremy asked us if we were ready to go in and meet everyone, and we said yes, but we have some things in the car.

He and Roger carried the bags for everyone in, and I carried Cindy and Chris's fruit basket in. I know you are wondering why the pineapple because the pineapple in Charleston means hospitality and friendship. I was thanking them for their hospitality and the friendship they were offering. They were so gracious and friendly; it was lovely talking to them. Cindy is now married to a man she knew in grade school; she was married to Jeremy's adopted father until he passed away in 2002 from cancer. We watched the girls open their presents for their birthdays and just being able to look at them in person. I had seen pictures of everyone, but this is so much more gratifying. Every time I looked at Jeremy, I see my own eyes looking back at me; what a different feeling that is. When he is talking to someone else, I see Roger's nose and chin; he is so big. And I laugh under my breath thinking, *Yep, that is what you get with a nine-pound, four-ounce baby.* He was laughing with Roger and then I really saw them, my dimples. Wow, I can really see me in him a lot of me, and a lot of Roger too. His eyes are blue like Roger's brother's, Mark, are and he has light brown hair now, but it was light blond; he was a towhead. We thought we would find a redheaded son with green eyes, but nope, we found a blue-eyed, son with brown hair. That was okay with us; there was no way anyone could ever deny; he is ours. He even talks with his hands like Roger does. Cindy surprised us by bringing Jeremy's baby book out to let us look at the pictures; what a generous lady she is. Roger and I both enjoyed the pictures of him growing up, and we could see the resemblance in these pictures.

Roger, Jeremy, and Chris went outside to look at Roger's car and then to look at the car Chris was building. The girls went out too; they were running around on the driveway when Sophie took a tumble because of her new flip-flops; she started crying and Roger was ready to run to her. When her daddy told her you are not dying, and I don't see any broken bones so come here. She went to her daddy, and he told her she would live but to go to her mom; she knew he could not understand what she was saying when she was crying. Then he told Ana to go with her to tell your mom what happened. When we heard them coming, we all jumped up to see what was wrong. Sophie was still crying, and Sara handled it all like the pro she is. She knew just how to make it better. When Roger told me this story. I could hear the amazement in his voice because of the way Jeremy handled it, not being around small children and delicate little princesses to boot, he just did not have a clue. GOD bless him; he will learn.

We went outside with the girls, and they stood on the well house in the front yard and sang songs to us; we videoed them. It was the best present we could have gotten from them. We spent most of the day with them having a light lunch, and later in the afternoon, Cindy, Sara, and I were sitting in the yard when they were talking about going to Disney. I told them I had never been to Disney, and they were flabbergasted. Sara immediately said, "You guys need to come with us." I told her I would ask Roger. She said, "Okay." Then later, she asked Roger herself, and he said okay, fine, if Betty wants to go. One other thing changed in my life that day. Ana got new earrings for her birthday from her grandma Cindy, and I asked her if she liked having her ears pierced, and she told me, "Yes, I do." I told her I had never pierced my ears and she told me, "You should get yours done."

I told her, "Next time you see me after tomorrow, I will have them done."

She replied, "That's good." Having more granddaughters was making my heart grow bigger; it is wonderful. Having my son to look at to touch is amazing. I feel sure my heart will mend even more now.

We all went out to dinner, and Jeremy sat between his mother and me; how lovely that was for us. I did not ask him. He is also exceedingly kind; he talked to us and everyone else while always keeping an eye on his girls. It was so wonderful to watch; he never yells. He just calls their names, and they understand that whatever they were doing they needed to stop. He did not make me nervous like most men do after I was around him a while and watched him interact with the girls. He is just wonderful in my book, and to me, that is all that counts.

We had a good time at dinner, but I do not know what I ate. It was all surreal, if you know what I mean. I was there participating in it all, but I was also watching from a distance too in my mind to soak up every nuance of what was happening. Holding it close to my heart and watching Roger too, I could see the difference in him already. He had a happy glow, not unlike the one we both had the first time we talked to Jeremy. He was like a proud papa with his son; if people he knew had walked into the restaurant, he would have stopped them and said, "Here, meet my son."

After dinner, we told them goodbye that we would see them for breakfast in the morning. We made plans to have breakfast with them and spend the day with them. We were exhausted not because of the day we had, but because of the emotional rollercoaster we had been on. We loved every minute we were there and would do it again in a heartbeat, but it was emotional. We knew it was going to take a while for us to come down off the high we had been on the whole day. We rode back to the hotel, telling each other things this one and that one had said. When we go back to my room, we got our selves some coffee and sat and talked and looked at the pictures we had taken and watched the videos we took of the girls.

I told Roger about Ana telling me to get my ears pierced and he just laughed and said, "See that you do get it done." Shortly thereafter we parted, and he went to his room, and I took a long hot soak in the tub. I knew that would help me relax. After saying my prayers and thanking GOD for this wonderful day, I lay there thanking HIM again. I was thinking about the fact that when you lose a child in death if you believe in GOD. You know that child is in heaven, but when you give a child up for adoption, you don't know where that child is and who is raising it and how. You wonder if the child is being treated right or if it is being mistreated; it is an extremely hard process to endure. Every day, you are reminded that your child is out there, and you have no contact or can ever know what is happening to him. I cannot express what it was like to meet him. Mourning for him all those years, making my peace with GOD because I had not met him here that I would meet him in heaven. I had no idea of the plans GOD had for Roger and me. Our GOD is so awesome, so loving and so giving, and again, I have learned you cannot out do GOD at any point in your life, when you believe in HIM and trust HIM.

The next morning, I was up and ready when Roger knocked on my door; we were out the door, and on our way immediately, with great anticipation, not like yesterday when we were flying blind, this was easier we all knew each other, and we were glad to go and see them again. Not that we were not glad yesterday; it was an awesome day that was painted in our hearts and minds forever. Today was going to be fun and more relaxed for everyone. We went to breakfast, and Sophie wanted to sit on the end.

Her dad said, "No, you sit here," and she was whining, and he looked at her and asked, "Sophie, what do we get when we whine?" She rolled her big blue eyes at her Grandpa Roger and said, "Nnootthhiinng," in her small southern voice. Roger's heart melted. He told me later, laughing, "It was just pitiful that *nothing*."

Watching him with the girls was a delight; he has no clue what to expect out of them, and sometimes their vocabulary just blows you away. You can tell they like to read just by their vocabulary, which is awesome. After breakfast, Cindy and Chris went back home to give us a chance to have some one-on-one time with them all. Again, I cannot express how wonderful they are, to put us first like that it is absolutely amazing. We went to the Children's Science Museum and let the girls go; they had to try everything we enjoyed it too, and we had time to talk to Jeremy and Sara while we all watched the girls.

Later we went to get lunch and an ice cream cones for the girls; we knew our time was about to end and that was okay; we knew we would see them again in October when we went to Disney. Reluctantly, we told them goodbye; they had to drive back to Knoxville that evening. We left them eating ice cream and told them we would see them later. It was not too hard because we were going to see them later.

How to tell you about the uplifting we got from spending time with them; they are a happy family, and I know that sounds corny to some people, but if you had ever lived in an unhappy family, you would know what I mean. Roger had a happy family growing up, and I had a happy family with my children and their father, but growing up in my family when I was a child, unfortunately, my dad made our life miserable, but when he was not around and we were with Mama, we always had fun, and we were all blessed because of the mother she was.

We went back to the hotel to rest a while, we talked about the conversations we had when we were apart with different ones. We each spent time with all of them one on one, and it was genuinely nice. I told him my stories and he told me his stories. It was a mutual sharing learning about the new family members in our life. Every now and then, we just sat there and smiled, and we knew what the other was thinking, what a magnificent gift we had been given. Thank you, GOD, amen!

We later went out for dinner, and he had a hamburger, and I had a turkey burger. I guess I should tell you I don't eat beef or pork, but I eat turkey, chicken, and fish because the doctor said eat some kind of meat or take iron shots, ouch! I worked it out, but I would rather eat just vegetables, fruits, grains, and nuts. The children cannot understand why my two favorite desserts are carrot cake and sweet potato pie. They all love chocolate except for Jeremy; he is not a big fan of chocolate, and neither are Roger and I. Roger and Jeremy love lemon meringue pie. I am so glad because I make a pretty nice one.

The next morning, we took it easy and checked out of our hotel rooms and then went to breakfast; again we were going slow and having some fun. We went toward Asheville and rode on the Parkway and visited a few shops. I was looking at some of the earrings wondering what kind I would wear when I got my ears pierced when Roger found me; he was like, "These are pretty." They were handmade ones from the local people. I agreed and he said, "This blue pair would look good on you." I told him yes, but they weren't pierced yet. He said, "We will get that fixed when we get to Charleston."

I thought, *Boy he is serious*, and then he said, "I will buy you these and these (which was a green pair) to keep you motivated," and he did. So I stopped looking at things.

We had a long drawn-out day, and while we rode, we talked to some in his family and some of mine telling them about our weekend and how wonderful it was. When we got back to the lake in Short Stay later, we had already had dinner, and I was not going back to Goose Creek for a few days. We made plans for the next day and decided that the first thing we would do after breakfast was go to the mall and get my ears pierced. Did I agree to that?

We are having dinner on Tuesday night at Bonnie and Karl's with Evelyn and Otto. I did not tell them I got my ears pierced just to see if they noticed. Bonnie had dinner ready when she got a call from Evelyn. She was late getting off work and could not come. She is a dialysis nurse. Therefore, I had to say something some I could tell them both at the same time. I had always told them if God wanted me to have hole in my ears. He would have put them there. So I told Evelyn ask Bonnie if she sees anything different about me, and Bonnie was looking for me over when Evelyn asked her, "Does she have a ring on her finger?" And I said, "No, it is not that." Then I put my hair behind my ears, and she said, "Oh my goodness, she has pierced her ears!" Then I told them about Ana and what she said, so Roger took me to get it done. They were like "You are fifty-eight years old and now you, do it?"

Roger answered and said, "Yes, she did."

Chapter 20

We went back to the lake. I had a room, and we had so much to still talk about. We were still riding the high of the weekend. Roger went upstairs and came back down and sat beside me on the sofa. He picked up my hand and put something in my palm and closed my fingers around it. When I opened my hand, I was amazed to see his class ring in my hand. Oh boy, he had never known how badly I wanted to wear that ring when we were dating all those years ago and why now was he showing it to me? I looked up at him with a question in my eyes and he said, "Will you marry me?"

Oh my stars, of course I said, "Yes." I could hardly believe it; see what God does? I had no clue that was where he was going with this, but I sure am glad. We were up late; we did not go to bed until the early hours.

The next morning, we had coffee and then went out and got breakfast. Then I had things to do. I had to go to my house and get some clothes for the following weekend. It was class reunion time. Today is Wednesday, and we had phone calls to make; first, Roger called Jeremy and said, "Jeremy, I'm going to marry your mother and I need a best man?"

Jeremy told him, "I'm there. When?"

Roger told him we did not know when, but he would let him know as soon as we knew.

I then dialed Cleo's number. Roger wanted to ask him for my hand. I heard the phone ring and heard Cleo's voice, and I said, "Cleo?"

His reply was, "Mama, what are you doing on the phone? I was talking to a store manager and now you are on here?"

I said, "I called you because Roger wants to talk to you. I handed him the phone, and he said, "Cleo?"

Cleo responded with "Yes, sir?"

Roger then asked him, "I would like your permission to marry your mother."

Cleo paused for a moment and told him, "Yes, sir, you sure can!"

Roger told him, "Thank you and I will take good care of her."

Roger then handed me the phone and I told Cleo, "I will let you know all the particulars later, son. We don't have anything set yet."

He said, "Yes, ma'am. Mama, but I need to go back to work and call that manager back."

I told him, "That's fine, I love you, bye."

Then I got to call Lori, and she was so excited for me. I cannot even remember all she said other than "That is great." She is so sweet. I knew she would be excited for her mama. She is always happy for other people to have good things happen to them. Even when she is having a hard time in her life, I have never seen or heard her begrudge other people their happiness. She totally gets that from my mother; anyone can call her and say "I need help," and she is there for you. The whole family knows that.

After I told my children I called my sisters, Bonnie was so happy and so was Evelyn; she was glad things were working out and that I would not get hurt. I told her, "No, we would be just fine." We arranged to have lunch with them all, except Ken and Pam on Thursday, Bonnie and Karl, Will, Kline, Bob, and Karen and Evelyn. The other spouses were working. We were going to Crazy Ds in Goose Creek. We walked in after everyone was there, and Roger stopped at the end of the table and made an announcement; looking at my brothers, he said, "I'm in love with your sister and I'm going to marry her and if anyone has an objection, let us take it outside."

There was silence and then everyone was congratulating us and shaking his hand; the ladies were telling him, "It is about time" and "Welcome to the family." I could have fainted when he said that last part. I was like "Are you crazy?" Later, I asked him about what he said. He told me, "I figured I could outrun them. They are all older than me." He is so funny!

I called Melinda, and we talked. She was so happy for me. I knew she would be. I had been widowed since 1998. and it was now 2010. She knew he was the right one and that it was time for me to get married. I was too young to be alone.

She told me, "Let me know when and where, and I'll be there."

I had never dated anyone since Carl passed away. I had no use for men. The funny thing is, Pastor Lindsay told Roger, "If anyone had told me that Betty was interested in a man, I would have told them that was not true. She does not even like men."

Everyone knew how I felt I did not need to tell them I guess it was obvious. I never played games with men like some women do; that is not my style. I did not want any one in my space; I had good friends, family members (cousins), and of course, my brothers. I loved them but everyone else I kept at a distance.

We had a full weekend ahead of us. When I say class reunion, I did not say we have a reunion for the first six classes that graduated from Goose Creek High School. That is how we did it we had so many siblings to graduate after us we just put them all together, the class of 1970 to 1975. Our younger siblings are coming too. Evelyn and Otto were coming and so were Mark and Sue too. At our age, we were all glad to be together.

Friday night, I got dressed and Roger came to pick me up. I knew the cat had been let out of the bag. Lori worked with her area manager (Jackie), and she was two years behind me in school, and one of the ladies was married to a guy that went to school with me. Lori told them I was getting married, and of course, I had put it on Facebook. I knew there was going to be a barrage of questions. When we walked into the school for the meet and greet, the people there did everything but dance in the foyer of the school. Lots of old friends, I was glad to see some of them I had not seen since the last reunion, five years before.

Because I was on the alumni committee, I had to go on stage with all the others that worked too, and they asked us each of us to tell them a little about what we had been doing since the last reunion. Boy, were they going to be surprised when I told them what I had been doing. I told them that Roger and I had looked for our son and had found him and had spent last weekend with him and his family. That when we came back home, Roger had asked me to marry him again, and I said yes. The room erupted with applause; everyone likes a happy ending. After the meet and greet, we went out with some of my friends for dinner and then left; tomorrow was going to be a long hot day. We went to the picnic, and it was hot. We pulled up in that red Corvette; it was hot too. Well, the guys thought so. It was a barbeque lunch with coleslaw and buns and some chicken too, so I ate as well. We had a good time, but this time, I did not stay to help clean up like I usually do. We had plans; my future husband was taking me to dinner my first date in years and years. We went to the Japanese restaurant where a group of people sit at the table and eat. Everyone was very nice, and we were all talking, and they asked us who we were and where we lived, it is a southern thing. If you are sharing a table, you usually talk to the people at the table; that's the way it is done in the south. We are very polite people; sometimes you run into a stinker and you just ignore them and everyone else has fun. When they asked, I told them I was on a date with this man for the first time in forty-two years; their mouths dropped open and all they said was, "Why?" We told them the abbreviated version of our story, and they were so happy for us, and we had a wonderful time.

The next morning, I got ready for church. Roger was coming with me; we have so much to be thankful for, and I wanted to tell my church family how GOD had answered my prayers. Not only had we met our son and his family; we had other news as well. I told them that Roger had asked me to marry him, and I said yes. Just like the reunion on Friday night, the church erupted in applause. Then Mr. Bob Brooks prayed for us and thanked GOD for the wonderful work he had done in our lives. I was in tears. I was so thankful for this church family and my life here. I knew I would be leaving, but not when. I was going to miss every one of them, and the children I taught in children's church.

After church, we went back to the lake for a while and then back to my house to get ready for the dance. We usually dress up for the dance, so I was ready with my outfit, and Roger was so handsome in his blazer and slacks. We were off to have a good time, the dance was held in a club on Myers Road in Goose Creek. I knew where it was and directed Roger there. We knew it was going to be fun the minute we drove in. You could hear the driving music outside as we exited the car, and the parking lot was packed. This place was hopping, we were going to dance; we did not dance a lot when we were dating because Roger was always singing. We danced sometimes at my house when he did not have a gig, and we had a date. I love to dance. I learned early. We all did well. Not Will so much, but the rest of my family dance anytime we can. I dance at my house when it is just me. We went in, and all our friends were there and some family. We got a table and then everyone that had not been at the picnic want to congratulate us on our engagement; it was so nice. Then we were dancing to be in his arms again; it was lovely.

We did not stay late, but we had good food, fun times with friends, and enjoyed the music. The next morning, Roger was leaving for his drive home; it would take him two days to drive home. I knew I would be on the phone with him while he was driving to keep him awake and know how things went.

The next morning, he came by my house to say goodbye; that took a little while, and then he was off. I was sad to see him go, but I would see him soon; he wanted me to come to Maine and see where I was going to live. He was going to get me a ticket when he got home, so I would be going at the end of July. He told me he would call me after he stopped to get gas for the car, so I was waiting. My phone rang, but it was not him; it was Bonnie. She was on her way to work; she asked me, "Is your honey gone?"

I said, "Yes, he just left. He is going to get gas and then be on his way."

She replied with "I thought so I just passed him at the gas station right before I turn off for work."

I said, "Don't worry. I'll be fine. I'm going to Maine at the end of July to see where I'm going to live."

Then she said, "I know you are excited to go, but I'm going to miss you."

I told her, "I know it's going to be hard, so I'm going a few times before we get married, and I've never been that far from my children and grandchildren for that long. It's got me a little scared, but trust me, I'm going."

Roger called a little while later; he was on the interstate highway and moving along, I told him to "be careful."

He replied, "I'm always careful," with a smile in his voice. I told him, "You forgot I have been in that car with you on the open road."

I was nagging and he just said, "Yeah, yeah!"

While I was on the phone with Roger, I asked him where he was staying that night, he said, "I don't know I did not book a place to stay tonight."

I asked him, "Do you want me to find you a place what town or city are you aiming for?" He told me where he wanted to stop, so I got off the phone with him and found him a room right on the interstate with breakfast so he could get on the road early. Then I called him back and told him the address so he could put it in his GPS. He got there safe and sound and had a good night's sleep. The next day, he was on the last leg of his trip. I know he was glad to go home. He loves that little red Corvette but riding in it a long time takes a lot out of you. We talked off and on all day, and he finally got there. He was going to work the next day at 2:00 p.m.; he had time to rest.

From time to time, we got to talk a long time, but sometimes he was working, and I was busy too. We were trying to pick a wedding day. Picking a wedding day is hard when you had a previous life; there are so many variables to think about, when was your previous anniversary, previous spouses' birthdays, things like that you don't want to hurt anyone's feelings. So we started going through the months and deciding which ones were available it took us to March the next year 2011. While we were talking about it, I asked Roger about Saturday, March 12, 2011. He thought that was okay. I then asked him if that was the day we were going to get married in 1968. He went and got the license, and it was. We applied for them on Friday, the eighth of March, and we were going to marry on the twelfth, but you know what happened. We were both excited to get married on the same day we were going to all those years ago.

Roger then did something that blew me away; he called the courthouse in Charleston, South Carolina, and asked if the license was still valid? He told them we were getting married to each other now and our previous spouses had passed away. They went to the judge in the courthouse, and he said, "They paid their $12. They can use them and to have fun."

That really amazed me. I had no clue they were useable after so long, but GOD works in mysterious ways.

Chapter 21

I was getting ready to go to Brunswick, Maine. I was nervous and excited and could not wait to see Roger. However I was also going to meet his first wife's children; all I wanted was them to like me. Roger cared about them, and I know he wanted me to care too. It was in their hands, not mine. I like everyone and can adapt to change. I just hoped they could too.

The day I flew out, I hugged my babies, Wesley, Nathan, and Chelsea. They were growing so fast. I knew I would see a change when I got home; they would be starting to school, another year of change. I flew From Charleston, South Carolina, to LaGuardia, New York, and from there to Portland, Maine. Roger was at the airport in Portland to pick me up. I was so happy to see him again as he was to see me. I flew into his arms right there in public, just like I would have done forty-two years ago. He had told me we had a ride ahead of us, and we did it took use about forty-five minutes to get my luggage and get to his house. The house was huge with four bedrooms and three and a half baths, two stories, and a full basement. My goodness, cleaning this house was going to be a chore after my small three-bedroom and one-bath house that was about 1,200 square feet. My house would fit into it three times. Oh well, I can do that a little work never hurt anyone. After we deposited my luggage in the guest room, he showed me the whole house.

A while later, he asked me if I would like to go over to Cheryl's (his stepdaughter) house to meet her, and I told him that would be lovely. She lived in the next town over that was separated by the river, not far at all. She was nice, and I could see that he loved her and that she loved him. Roger had been around since she was about fourteen years old. Roger's first wife was older than he was, and her children were teenagers or grown when they got married.

He loved all of them, and I could tell by the way he talked about them and his relationships with all three of them. The guys were more his friends, not a stepfather-stepson relationship, but not Cher as he calls her. He told me she even did daddy duty when she went into the navy, just like the proud daddy he is!.

When we left Cheryl's house, he drove me around town so I could understand the layout of the town, but he also told me there was a GPS in his truck that I would be driving; that made me feel a lot safer. I knew I would be able to find home. We got some dinner, then we went home. I was tired. I did not sleep well the night before. I never do when I am traveling. I'm continually thinking about what I forgot to pack, even though I write a list and check it off as I go.

The next day was Sunday; we had a late breakfast and sat around, taking it easy. I was getting used to being in a different house. Roger kept saying, "This is your house now." I knew he was trying to make me as comfortable as possible, but I can say I did not feel like I was in another woman's home. I guess when you have experienced the death of a spouse you look at things different. I knew some people in my life that hated the thought of another woman living in the house that was going to be their home, or I should say a former spouse. It did not bother me. I was okay. In our case, the dead cannot hurt you. Anyway, we rested the whole day, talking without a telephone to our ears; it was so nice. Before bed, I asked him if he had plans for us the next day, and he said, "Yes, we were going for a ride to see the beautiful countryside."

I told him, "That is fine with me. I like sightseeing," and I knew we would have fun.

When I went downstairs the next morning, he was dressed and drinking coffee, I soon had a cup in my hand and was feeling better for a good night sleep. The only thing was he had a Keurig coffee maker. I usually had a whole pot of coffee. I was going to have to get use to this. I asked him about it; he said, "There in a coffee maker in the cabinet if you want to use it." After breakfast, I went back upstairs and got ready for the day of sightseeing; he makes me laugh so much, I just love being in his company. He was always fun, but now, he is full of fun and a lot of it has to do with him being in the navy for thirty years.

We were finally off for the day, and I had no idea where we were going, and I did not care. I was in good hands, so I went along for the ride. He was driving the Corvette and the day was beautiful, and all I had to do was fill my vision with the vistas we were seeing; some of them were breathtaking. He turned off on a side road and I asked him, "Where are we?"

He said, "I want to show me something and I think you will enjoy it."

It was a harbor, and it was beautiful. I did not know which way to look; he showed me the lobster traps in the water, and then told me the name of the place was Five Islands Harbor, then he pointed out the different islands to me. There was also a restaurant or cookery there that sold fresh boiled lobster. I knew then what he was going to eat, but not me. I do not care for lobster or shellfish. I eat mostly flounder or tuna. He said, "Excuse me a minute. I need to get something from the car."

I said, "Okay, I'm fine," and I was I was sitting on a rock on the edge of the water, drinking in the lovely setting.

When Roger came back from the car, I had my eyes closed listening to the background noises, when he said, "I brought you something."

It was a hat. I told him, "I am fine," and he insisted I needed the hat so I would not get sun-burned. So I took the hat and there was something in the hat. Oh my goodness, it was a ring box. I just stared at it, wondering what was inside, and then he said, "Open it."

I did. I could tell he was anxious. He was watching me like a hawk, and when I got it open, all I could do was gasp. It is huge and not only one but three diamonds. He had asked me what kind of ring I wanted, and I was with Evelyn so I handed her the phone and she told him what I said—three diamonds, one for the past, one for the present, and one for the future and in yellow gold. I could hardly take it in; he bought three huge diamonds, and it is gorgeous. But I felt bad. I said three. I thought three little ones but not him. If he had gotten one, it would have been bigger than my finger. I was almost scared to wear it, and then he kissed me and said, "Will you marry me?"

Of course I said "Yes" again, and then he slid it on my finger. There was a photographer there, so we asked her to take some pictures of him putting the ring on my finger and him asking me to marry me on his knee; it was perfect and just like a story book engagement.

We had lunch out and then we drove around, but nothing could compare to my vision of Five Islands Harbor; it will always be special to me, and the way he planned it. Sometimes it is the little things that you love the best. Do not get me wrong; the ring is gorgeous and big, but the fact he planned the special place and the special way he did it makes me love him more all the more! To have a man that plans things like that or just taking you out to eat without telling you ahead of time, he just says "Let's go for a ride" and then we ride and have dinner and listen to the music is wonderful. So many men want to know where. Do you want to go what you want to eat and we ladies sometimes just like a surprise. I have a special man, and on top of that, he makes me laugh.

Being with Roger has changed my life in a whole new way. I have always tried to take care of my children, Carl, when he was alive, my mother, and anyone else that needed me. Roger wants to take care of me. I want to take care of him; go figure. We are two of a kind. Maybe it is because we have both lost loved ones, but no one has ever taken care of me like he wants to. I do not daresay I want something because if it is feasible; he will try to get it. I try to make dinners he likes, and I do the laundry while I am here and clean the house. Our days are unusual; he goes to work around 1:00 p.m. so he takes a brief nap while I finish dinner and pack it for him to eat later, with snacks when he gets to work and make his afternoon tea. He likes hot tea and biscuits around 5:00 p.m. He is gone until he gets off at midnight. I get my shower and get ready for bed before he calls me on his way home, and he calls me when he eats his lunch too. That is four days a week; the other three days, we go places and shop.

We were trying to decide where to have the wedding, and I asked him if he had a preference and he said no just somewhere big enough for everyone. So we are getting married on Saturday, March 12, 2011, if we can find a venue large enough for all our guest. Once we figured out what time and where the wedding was going to be, we sent invitations to each person we wanted to be in our wedding, asking them if they would be in our wedding,;they all said yes with the exception of Logan. He said, "No." Logan and Hunter are the sons of Cleo's best friends, Audie and Jackie Tillman; these are grandchildren of my heart, and their parents are just like my kids. His mother asked him why he did not want to be in Mama's wedding; he told her in a crying voice, "I DON'T WANT TO GET MARRIED." I can be glad he still loves me; she told him he was the ring bearer and that was all he need only carry the pillow with rings on it and if he asked nicely Mama might give him the pillow; he was good with that, and of course, Mama gave him the pillow just like she used to hide chocolate for him when he was a toddler.

We were looking for patterns and fabric for the flower girls and groomsmen. I am making seven dresses for the girls and five vests and bowties for the little groomsmen. I know I am going to be quite busy until March 12, 2011, when we get married. That's okay. I love to sew, and it is easier to make them and not try to find dresses in the same color palette and basic style. I want them to have, and I don't want their parents or grandparents paying for them. This resolves that problem I did, however, I asked Sophie and Ana if they liked the patterns and they both colored them and let me know the design they wanted. Two of the dresses were going to be white: one with blue accents that was Sophie's and the other was solid white that was Caroline's (Roger's great-niece). She was the flower girl. There were four bigger girls that had blue dresses with white trim with a blue or white flower accent on them.

Lori, my daughter, was my matron of honor, and her dress was a long blue dress with white accents. The five young gentlemen were wearing vest and bowties the same color of the dresses but done in brocade fabric. I was ready to sew. They are Wesley and Nathan (my grandsons), Hunter, and Logan (grandsons of my heart) and Hilton

(Rogers great nephew). These guys are all everyone stinkers and full of mischief. They will make great ushers and groomsmen and ring-bearer. Then we have our son, Jeremy, who is his father's best man, and TJ (Roger's great-nephew who is grown), and my son Cleo who gave me away. It is going to be a very large wedding with all the beautiful girls and all the handsome guys.

We got all the fabric ordered and patterns found before it was time for me to go home in September, so I could take it with me. Then I started cooking, making meals, and dividing them up and putting them in the freezer for Roger to eat while I was gone. It was all a part of me taking care of him.

Chapter 22

September 13 came all too soon, and it was time for me to go home. I had lots to do, and I was going to be very busy getting ready for Christmas—yes, Christmas. It is a lot of work when you are on a budget and want the children to get what they prefer. They are cautious in what they ask for, and I appreciate that, they know I do the best I can.

I was so glad to see my grandchildren. I had never been apart from them for that long, or Cleo and Lori either; it really tugs at your heart when you don't see those smiling faces. They think you are perfect, and that is very humbling. Being gone was a good test for me. I was learning what being apart from them was going to be like.

I was still talking to Roger just like I did before I went to Maine. He told me when I came back in November we were going to go shopping for my dress. At first, I told him I would make it, and he said, "No, you will buy it, you have enough sewing to do already." He would not budge from that, so I relented and told him, "Okay, we would find one when I came back in early November." That is him taking care of me.

I was getting things ready for our trip to Disney World. Roger was going to fly to Charleston, and he is going to rent a car and drive to Orlando. This is the second week of October. We are so excited about spending time with Jeremy, Sara, and the girls. Cindy and Chris were coming and so were Sara's parents. We needed costumes for the Halloween party at Disney, Mickey's Not-so-Scary Halloween. We are going dressed as farmers in overall and flannel shirts with straw hats.

Time was flying by, and my grandchildren were growing so fast; it seemed when I got home. They were taller and bigger. Truly, they were, and they needed more clothes for the coming fall, and I was ready to get them some, so I did some shopping for that. I get up every morning with them and helped them get ready for school. Sometimes Nathan struggles in the morning, and I go out on the porch with him, and he gets inside my robe, and I hold him so he can rest on me till I see the bus coming. I enjoy holding him, and he needs his Mama sometimes and Mama needs him. Wesley is outside with his friends waiting on the bus, but not my little one. Wesley is more outgoing than Nathan, but that is okay. All God's children are different, and I love them all equally. Just like I always loved my children.

Roger flew into Charleston and rented a car, and we were off to Disney World. We were getting there a day later than the rest of them. Roger had to work, and we were going as far as Jacksonville the first night then to Orlando the next morning.

We were staying with Cindy and Chris at their condo, so we bought them their tickets to get into Disney. It was a nice trade, and we did not have to find rooms at a hotel, the places were packed. Roger nor I had ever been to Disney, so we did not know what to expect. Everyone was so nice and friendly; it was a joy to meet Dave and Marylee (Sara's parents); they are lovely people. The girls were making out too; they had three sets of grandparents with them at Disney. We found out that Ana had to have a secret from her class, and her secret was she has three sets of grandparents. We spent hours at Disney each day. I think Jeremy likes Disney better than anyone. He lets himself relax and have a good time. When the people at Disney found out we were engaged, they gave us pins to wear; even the ghost going into the haunted house asked me why I was marrying Roger.

I had to laugh and tell her, "He was my childhood sweetheart."

The night we went to the Olive Garden for dinner, we were waiting outside; it was a lovely evening, and the girls were restless so Ana came over to her Grandpa Roger and got into his lap to talk to him, watching his face was amazing. He had never had an experience like that; she was telling him something, and she was whispering in his ear, and I could tell by the look on his face his heart was falling further and further in love. I was so proud of this moment for him; I had to look at someone else so I would not cry.

I rode a rollercoaster for the first time. I was nervous about it, but Jeremy said, "Come on, you will be fine." I thought "I hope so," and he rode too just to make me feel better. We did other things we had never done before like riding dragons in the Harry Potter part of the park. While we were there, Roger asked Jeremy if he could buy the girls something special, and he told him that was fine. So he let them pick and Ana and Sophie got a scarf in the colors that the Gryffindor students wore.

Saturday morning, we were telling everyone goodbye, and we would see them in March for our big day; they were all coming to the wedding. Roger and I drove off full of love and kisses and best wishes. We went as far as Jacksonville; when we got there, we went shopping, and he bought me a diamond necklace to wear with my wedding gown that I did not have yet. He overwhelms me when he does things like that.

He makes me feel like a princess. I have never felt like that before. The next morning, I was ready to go when he was, and we got on the road to Charleston right after we found some breakfast. The drive to was nice after we got to the exit at Point South, South Carolina, and on 17N. When we got to my house, we took my stuff in and then did some visiting with his family. He was flying home the next morning; he had to go to work on Tuesday. Later that evening, before going to his hotel we sat and talked about how much we enjoyed Disney with everyone and meeting everyone. We had a wonderful time. The next morning, he came by my house, and I followed him to the airport, just like last time he flew to Maine.

Our lives have changed so much in the last nine months; it was amazing. Before he left, he told me he would book me another ticket to Maine as soon as he got home; we have a dress to find for you. There he goes again fixing things for me, and I love him for it, but he does too much I think and said so and he said, "No, never."

I did not argue with him he was leaving shortly, and I am going to miss him, so I kissed him instead. Then I kissed him goodbye when he went to the security gate. He called me during his stopover in New York. Then he called again while he was driving home from Portland to Brunswick. I told him when he got home to get some dinner and rest, and of course, I told him I already missed him. He told me to think about when I wanted to fly back up to Maine, and tomorrow, he would book my ticket.

Have you ever gone wedding dress shopping with the man you are going to marry? Well, it was a lot of fun. I was sure this was something I needed to do by myself or with my sisters, but he wants to help. Then he asked me, "Who do you think will tell you what looks best on you and who do you ask all the time do I look okay?"

He was right, and he has excellent taste, and he knows what he likes and other than me who should we please. It was hilarious. We went from store to store in the freezing cold and snow in Maine. I tried on dresses we liked, some I liked and some he liked and some that were recommendations from the salesperson. I guess because I was turning sixty made me think twice about the color, and he was adamant that I needed to wear white, so I did. That was what we finally chose. We went to all the little towns around Brunswick to every bridal shop they had.

We found lots of laughs. I would put on some of the dresses, and I looked so funny when my eyes met his in the mirror, all he did was shake his head. I guess the ladies in the store thought I should dress like an old woman, but I was not ready to be old, and neither was he. We went to Portland and found some shops with the same dresses we saw everywhere else, and then we found a listing for a boutique called "Marisa Antonietta Couture." We made an appointment to see what she had. Her inventory was lovely and different, not like the ones you see in every shop. I looked around and found one that was gorgeous, a plain satin princess-style with a natural waist. It was perfect but I needed to try it on and then I saw the price tag $859.

I turned away. I thought, *No*. Roger was standing there and said, "Try it on," and I told him, "No, it costs too much."

He said, "Try it on anyway."

The owner saw us looking at it and told us about the dress; it was made in New York City by a Russian designer, and it was now on sale for half price.

Roger told her, "Please let her try this one," and she obliged. It is meticulously made and beautiful, and I felt like a dream in it. When I went out of the dressing room, Roger's face said it all. I loved it, and so did he. The only drawback is that it is sleeveless, and I wanted sleeves. When I told the saleslady, she brought out a sheer silky wrap that goes over the shoulders and hangs down in points in front; it was perfect, just enough covering. She also suggested we add a little lace to the dress; she was thinking at the waist, and I told her lace yes, but vertical down one side. She held the lace up to the dress, and it was a wonderful dream come true. We purchased the dress and left it with her to add the lace and have her make me a shawl like the one she showed me; she was wonderful. That was a wonderful day. Roger was determined that I was going to buy that dress and we did.

The next week, he told me we needed to go car shopping, and I was like, "What?"

Then he said, "You need your own car. I like driving my truck and you need a car."

So off we went to look at the ones he thought I should have; there were three different kinds, a Toyota RAV4, a Toyota Highlander, and a Lexus 400h. We drove all of them, then he asked me, "Which one do you want?" I was stunned. I did not know anything about cars and what they cost. I had been driving a Neon that was bought before Carl died in 1998. I asked about the price, and he told me they were all about the same. I did not care for the RAV4, so it was between the Highlander and the Lexus. When we drove the Lexus, we drove it into a parking lot at the mall and decided we should check out the back seat. We got in the backseat, and it was comfortable, so we went to get out, and we were locked into the backseat. We started laughing, and it took us forever to stop. We were like why did this not happen to us forty-one years ago? The child locks were engaged; it was hilarious I had to climb between the front seats and get to the front and get us out. It was not easy. I was not a size 2, way bigger than that. So I got a Bamboo Green Lexus with all the bells and whistles; it is a hybrid and a dream to drive.

I will be in Maine for a few more weeks until I got the house decorated for him; last year he had a little ceramic tree and nothing else. Well, not this year. I would decorate his house and then go home and decorate mine; this was the last Christmas I would spend with my children and grandchildren, and I was going to make a big deal out of it. I was going to decorate, cook, and do all their favorite things. Just thinking about it being my last Christmas with them made me weep, but I knew we would get through it, and it would get better, and I would be with Roger. We ordered Christmas presents for Jeremy and his family from LL Bean's, which was easy we let them, or should I say, Sara pick out things for them, and I made the a few things for them. I shopped for Roger and Cheryl while I was still in Maine, so I did not have to ship things back there, and then I was free to concentrate on the kids when I got home.

I went home just before my birthday, which was the day before Thanksgiving. For my birthday, Roger sent me a machine that has a record player, tape player, and a CD player that you can transfer your music from the record and tape player to a CD. I had told him about them and asked if he had one, and I promise that was all I said. As usual, he was listening and got it for me. I was thrilled. Music, if I had not said before, is like dessert for my soul. I love music, all kinds. I am one of those people that hears a song, and I am like, "Listen and grab my heart," and the hair stands up on my body.

It was going to be a long month till I could go back to Maine in January but needs must. Besides, the children and grands, this was going to my last Christmas with my siblings too; we are a very close family, and we like to see each other on the holidays, and as often as we can. This, too, was going to be an adjustment for me; we generally try to get together and have lunch during the holiday if we can. We always reach out with phone calls on Christmas Day, to see how everyone faired for Christmas, even when you do not have a lot of money. We have lots of love and caring. We all know the real meaning of Christmas and that is the important part. So yes, we love like JESUS said, and our mother taught us to love each other until Mama passed away in 1991. We spent every Christmas Eve at her house, all seven of us and our families. It was such happy chaos. If the walls of that house could talk, they would have a lot to say. I also had a lot of friends at my church, and we always had some Christmas gatherings that were fun and inspiring too. I want to marry Roger, and I am going to marry Roger because I love him like I love no one else. I'm just saying my life is going to change in a really big way, and soon, in three and a half months.

Christmas with the with the children is wonderful; they were all happy with what they got and eager to give the presents they bought for us and each other. I have always taught them it is more fun to buy for someone else than to get something. I talk to them about what they want to buy each other and then take them shopping alone. Then when I take them shopping for their mom and Henry, their stepfather, I take them to the dollar store and give them some money, and they never buy anything for themselves. They buy for their mom and Henry, and sometimes they buy me a secret gift, just from them. I spent time with my siblings and talked to everyone I love. They all had a great Christmas even the old curmudgeons; you know the ones that say I don't like Christmas, you just have to spend money. They had a good Christmas too. Now I can tell you what Roger got me. He took me shopping at LL Bean's and bought me clothes, an all-weather jacket in green, of course, slacks, shirts, a vest, and plaid PJs. I had to leave some of my old stuff there so I could bring my new stuff home. All of us thanked GOD our FATHER for the BLESSING of HIS SON at the anniversary of HIS birth. We are aware what it would mean for us if JESUS had not been born and SAVED us from our sins.

This New Year's Day was quite different from last year when I sat at my computer and entered all our information about Jeremy in the reunion sites. Just talking about the change in our lives brought Roger and me to tears; the magnificent gifts we had been given was not lost on us. We are well and truly extremely thankful for all of it. The fact that Jeremy and his family is in our lives and that we are going to get married was not something we ever imagined would happen. We can see the miracles just like everyone else.

Chapter 23

On January 13, 2011, I went back to Maine; the first thing we did was assemble the wedding invitations and get them in the mail; that way, they were there two months before the wedding. They were stunning. Sara had taken the information we had written and designed them and ordered them, and she had taken a picture of us when we were in Disney and inserted a picture of us from the Sweetheart banquet of 1967. The whole theme of our wedding was "Some Things Are Meant to Be." We got that done, and I packed all the wedding things I had sent to his house for him to bring down when he comes.

Then I still need to finish up the sewing I was doing there, and when I get home again, I will finish up the dresses I am making there. I had stuff from pillar to post, and when I go back to Charleston, I need to finish the final touches of the wedding supplies and things for the reception. I was not staying long in Maine. I was finishing up Sophie and Ana's dresses, and some of the vest and bowties for the boys. The other five dresses were at my house in Goose Creek, South Carolina, waiting for the final touches; to say I was busy was an understatement. While I was there, Roger's naval dress uniform came in, and I had to alter that too. You know, hem the pants, shorten the sleeves, and sew on that row of stripes that was almost as long as his sleeve. We picked up my dress and debated how to get it to my house; in the end, we decided that Roger could bring it down when he drove down. I did not want to travel with it.

I cooked for Roger again, making dinners for the freezer, like I did last time, so he did not have to eat can soup and fast food. Then it was time for me to go back to Charleston. It was the middle of February, and we had a month to go before the big day, and I needed time to bring everything together. He sent me off with a kiss and a smile, telling me he would be there the week before. What I have not told you is he also booked us a Mediterranean cruise for our honeymoon, but we are coming back to Maine after the wedding in March and going on our honeymoon at the end of April. We thought it best to wait a while after all the traveling back and forth for the wedding to go that far and that long. I also sent Ana and Sophie their dresses so we knew they would fit, and they did. Thank goodness.

When I got home, I had to get in the fast mode. I finished up the dresses and vest and bowties, delivered all that had to be delivered. Went to Bonnie's and we finished making the bouquets for all the girls to carry. Karl took a basket Bonnie had and spray-painted it white so I could put all the bouquets in it. I decided they needed to carry silk flowers and not real ones. They carried white daffodils with yellow throats. Caroline is going to carry flower petals in a basket that I made for her, and Sophie is carrying yellow daffodils like me. I had ordered my flowers and the boutonnieres for the men and boys and flowers for the church. I had to shop for the shoes I was going to wear, and I had not found a wedding cake topper yet. Roger did not need a boutonniere his uniform had so many medals and ribbon on it, he had more jewelry than me, and I had the diamond necklace he bought me in Florida and a beautiful dressy watch and a stunning pair of diamond earring he bought me to wear with my dress.

As the days got closer, the more I got things done, the better I felt, and Lori was helping me continue to pack my belongings I was taking with me. My sewing machine and books most everything else I gave to Lori because Roger's house is already full of things. My furniture dishes pots and pans, I did not need even the linens for the beds were different sizes. I was unpacking my dresser where I kept important papers when I found the information I had compiled in 1989 when I was searching for Jeremy. As I went through it, I found the stenographers pad I used in the courthouse while searching. I flipped it open, and I had a list of numbers with the corresponding names on the following pages. There in black-and-white were the names of Jeremy's parents and his full name too. I could hardly breathe. It shows you in a very real way that it has to be when GOD is ready, not us humans. In GOD's time is when it happened. I learned a long time ago that things do not make you happy anyway, it is your relationship with the Lord that makes you happy in this world and your love ones. Everything I have encountered in this life even when I've been at the hardest and darkest times it was the Lord that helped me through, or should I say, it's my belief in Him that brought me through. Because I believe in Him and His promises. I know I can continue to live and deal with life here because I am just a visitor here and my home is with Him in heaven.

Roger still calls me every day, and we continue to talk throughout the day when he is off. When he is working is when I get most of my things completed. I went shopping and found my shoes and everything else I needed for myself. I knew we had more things to do when he got here, we had gift boxes to fill with candy for our guest.

He was bringing some of the other things we ordered with him, like the napkins for the cake table and our guest book. I will be glad when he is here. I still have not found a cake topper, but we will, I am sure.

The ladies at the church had me a wonderful shower at Pastor and Debbie's house; it was a lot of fun, and the gifts were lovely—things we could really use. My family had also had me a shower at Evelyn's house; and with Lori my sisters, sisters-in-law, nieces, cousins, and Aunt Marylou, there it was fabulous. You cannot put all of us in one room and not have fun. We laugh and tease each other and have a ball; we are all close and love each other. There is a lot to say about having a loving family. I see people so hurt by family members and it makes my heart hurt. I just want to tell them beware the next time you see them, or they see you it might be at theirs or your funeral then you cannot say "I'm sorry I hurt you" or "I did not act like I loved you." There will be broken hearts over what stuff, and the mean things you said or were said to you. Sometimes you just have to let it go and love people anyway. There is not a person in my family that I do not love. I love them all.

Chapter 24

The days were getting longer at the end of February like they do every year, and I knew it would not be long before Roger left Maine to drive down to South Carolina. He was going to stay at Short Stay again on the water. Most of his family was out that way too, and I knew he would visit with them. We had received RSVPs from almost everyone we invited; it was going to be a good time. Everything I could think of was almost done; we invited all the wedding party to the rehearsal and the people helping me. Linda Parker, Bonnie's friend, was our director; she was in control of the children and when who did what. They were all invited to the rehearsal dinner at Kelly's Barbecue with all the out-of-town guests too. We invited the ladies and the girls of the wedding party and the out-of-town women to the church for a luncheon at noon on the day of the wedding. Jeremy arranged for the men of the wedding party and out the male members from the out-of-town guests to lunch together with Roger and him in downtown Charleston. I was trying to stay on top of everything so no one would get their feelings hurt; that is the last thing we wanted.

    I could literally see time moving faster and faster, only when I got some quiet time and was by myself did I slow down enough to think about what is happening. To understand the big changes that were going to take place in my life, thanking GOD every day for those changes and the blessings HE has given me.

    Roger was working the first week of March and then driving down on Saturday the fifth and Sunday the sixth. I was still getting things done; it never seemed to be finished. Something else would crop up. I moved all my things to a storage unit, and I went to stay with Bonnie and Karl that last week. Lori had moved back into the house because her apartment got flooded. She was trying to find another place to live and trying to keep her things in one place. It was easier for me to be out of the way. That way, after the wedding when we get the trailer, we rented we would just go to the storage place and load everything up.

Roger packed the Lexus ahead of time and drove his truck to work that way he would come home Friday night go to bed and get up the next morning and get on the road. He will be tired when he gets here. I know that it will take him a week to recover for the wedding, and we still have things to do. We have to deliver the things we bought for the wedding to the Redbank Club, get my dress out of the bag, and hung up so I can steam it if needed and make sure his uniform does not need to be pressed. Oh, and we need to find a wedding cake topper still or make one we like.

It was Saturday the fifth of March, and when he got on the road, he called me; the first part of his ride will be on I-95. I usually talk to him when he is on the road unless the traffic gets bad, then I let him go and concentrate on the road. My car had Bluetooth, so he does not even have to touch his phone; he just talks to the car, and it calls me; how cool is that? We talked for a long time, then he stopped for lunch and gas. I had some things to do, and I went to see Wesley and Nathan at the house. Then I was back talking to Roger later in the afternoon until he was ready to stop for the night; he was staying with some friends of his who are his first wife Irene's in-laws.

I knew he would be busy all evening visiting with his friends. I took that time to get some more things for the wedding and my leaving done. I had to fill out change of address forms on the computer. I have already contacted my doctors and had my records ready to be transferred. I had medicine filled at the Walmart in Maine, so they were ready to be transferred. I applied for a passport, never had one before; it will need to have a name change after we get married. Roger called me when he was getting ready for bed to tell me good night and told me he would call when he got on the road the next morning. I was excited he would be here tomorrow night depending on traffic.

He made good time all around; he even stopped at Tom and Ida's on his way in. They had come from Texas for the wedding, and there was a family get-together in the front yard at their place. Roger called Tom to see if they were there yet and they were, so he took a detour by there. I am glad he did he has not seen them in a while so it was all good; he told me he would be a little later than expected and that was fine. I am glad he has a good relationship with his family; it is so important. It is bad enough when your parents die, but when you have siblings, at least you have someone you can talk to who understands, someone who grew up in the same house and has the same memories.

He got to Bonnie's late Sunday afternoon, and we stayed around for a while and talked and had coffee, then we went to Short Stay. I needed to help him unpack the car. My wedding dress, his uniform, and separate the things we had to deliver. After we unloaded the car, we went for dinner and came back so he could go to bed. I told him good night so he would go to bed and rest. I could read and be quiet so he could sleep and rest. I got my clothes ready for the next day and went to bed shortly thereafter. We had a lot of things to do the next day, just about every day, until the wedding my mind was on a wheel spinning around and around, so I made a list of all the things we had to do on my phone; that way, I would not lose it. After making the list, I was able to go to sleep. I heard him get in the shower the next morning. I got up shortly after he went downstairs. I got dressed and met him downstairs; he looked like he had rested well and was ready to go for coffee and breakfast, and so was I.

We had breakfast in Moncks Corner at Howards Restaurant, a quaint little place by the railroad tracks. The coffee and breakfast came out hot and delicious. The waitress decided that my name was Hot Red, and that's not something new for me a lot of people that don't know my name call me Red because of my red hair, and it is red and will be red until the Lord calls me home. Roger told me one time because he was the redhead in his family, the guy at the ice-cream shop would always say to him, "So what are you having, Red?" His mother called him Red a lot of the times too.

We went to Walmart and got some things we needed there, and then we were off to Goose Creek; we went to make sure the trailer would be ready the next Monday, and we were assured it would be. Then went to Michael's to look for a cake topper, and as we were going in, we stopped to let a lady come out, and it was my old friend Tricia. She looked like she was seeing a ghost. I said, "Hello, Tricia," and she blinked and questioned, "Betty?"

And I said, "Yes," then she looked at Roger and was amazed.

She asked, "What are you all doing?"

And we explained we were looking for a cake topper for our wedding on Saturday, and we had to explain a lot of things. She then told us she worked there and would go back in and help us. So I can tell you my old friend made our cake topper and did a beautiful job.

As the week progressed, we were able to see to most of the things we had to do, and we were feeling good about that. We went to Bonnie's to fill the candy boxes he brought with him from Maine. After Valentine's Day, I went to the drugstore and bought a lot of valentine chocolates that here hearts and kisses I knew they would be perfect for our gift boxes to our guest,.Karl just wanted to eat the chocolate. We let him have some; we had plenty.

On Friday, the guys had to go pick up their tuxedos, and we had to pick up the tuxedo shirts for the little guys; that way, they all had the same type to go with black dress pants and their vests and bowties. I made them. That had to be done early because the rehearsal was at six o'clock and then the rehearsal dinner at Kelly's Barbecue.

We laughed through the rehearsal and had a good time. They all did their part just like they were supposed to, except me. I let Evelyn take my place going down the aisle, which is right and proper. I will wait for the big day to do that. Linda was wonderful with the children, and they all did good jobs; she knew what she was doing. Bonnie and Ida (Roger's sister-in-law) are going to light the candles in the church, so when it was all said and done, we knew it was going to be a beautiful wedding. Just one snag, we had to make a video that night of pictures of Roger and me during our growing up years, and the two of us together way back when. Good thing we had pictures on our phones. Then we had to add music to the video the first song was Roger singing to me, "You're Sixteen You're Beautiful and You Are Mine," and then we added, "Remember When?" by the Platters. It could not have worked out better. Roger singing was just beautiful, and I really enjoy The Platters. So tomorrow is another day. The biggest day since having my children and finding Jeremy; now I am marrying his father, and we have come full circle. It is amazingly wonderful how GOD orchestrates our lives, and we have no idea what is coming. We plan our life to go one way and HE sends us in another direction.

The luncheon the next day at noon was wonderful. The Kellys gave me the luncheon for my wedding present, and it was perfect. We had chicken salad croissants, fixings with iced tea, and lemonade. Perfect for such a busy day. Once I got to the church that day, I never left; after the luncheon, we had to decorate the sanctuary and make sure all the flowers were there and start getting people ready. When Roger and Jeremy got back from downtown, they helped the boys get ready. I was doing Chelsea's hair, then it was time for me to get dressed and the photographer was there taking pictures. His name is Clyde McDonald, and he was doing an excellent job. I had seen his work before, and I knew what to expect.

Chapter 25

I am sitting in the fellowship hall waiting for all the people to arrive. The guest to our wedding and the principal players in this saga. They are all going to be there, and this is the story you just read, and I am marrying Roger; it is a long time coming; forty-three years, in fact, but as far as I am concerned, better late than never. After all we have been through, I still love him, and he still loves me.

This whole story is a GOD-ordained story; the things that have happened and the way they happened came from a greater power than just humans. I know this deep in my soul. The thing I can tell you is, when you are a child of GOD, you automatically thank HIM all the time for your blessings, every day I thank HIM for Cleo and Lori and their families, for Jeremy and his family and for my love for Roger and his love for me. This coming full circle was all GOD's idea; it is a dream I never dreamed of. So I give all the glory to GOD for these miracles. What an AWESOME GOD and SAVIOR we have.

Linda came and got me after my long wait, Cleo was waiting to walk me down the aisle. He looked so handsome so much like his father. I thanked GOD again for the man he is and for his father too. When I got to the door of the church, I saw Lori on one side with the girls and Roger and Jeremy on the other side with all the boys; it was a beautiful sight. I was ready to start the rest of my life. The wedding went perfectly; everyone did what they were supposed to do just like they practiced last night, except I was the main player that was missing before, and I took my place beside the man I loved and was destined to marry just not when we thought all those years ago. TO GOD BE THE GLORY.

The whole thing was beautiful; when we got to the part where they were watching the video Pastor Lindsay had all the attendants sit down on the front row, and Roger and I stood off to one side watching the video, each other, and the guests. Pastor Lindsay introduced the video with a short message and then said, "The first song is by yours truly," meaning Roger. It sounded wonderful just like it did all those years ago. After that, we were pronounced man and wife and then Mr. and Mrs. Roger Matthews Hilton.

We left the sanctuary with big smiles on our faces, and then we got in line with all our attendants and Pastor Lindsay; the children were ready to shake hands with everyone. It was a long line, and as soon as people got threw the line, they we leaving for the reception venue. The reception was at the Redbank Club, near the Naval Weapons Station gate on, Redbank Road. When we got done with all the congratulations, we had to sign our marriage license that were forty-three years old. We were extremely glad to sign them; they had our names just like they were before, as though nothing had changed. But believe me, things had changed. We were adults now, and we both had particularly good marriages before, and we had lost our loved ones, so it was easy for us to get married again. We had no bad feelings or regrets about our other lives; now we are ready to start our new lives together.

We went outside the church; our white stretch limousine was waiting for us. As we got close to the car, we could hear the children. Yes, we are taking all the children with us in the limousine. We gave them sparkling white grape juice in plastic champagne glasses, and they drank it before we left so no one would spill it. They thought they were something else; we knew they would tell all their friends, and they would always remember this wedding. They did fine; they were all talking and giggling but trying to act grown-up until we got to the first red light. Then I told them they could see the people outside our limo, but the people could not see them. They changed in an instant; they started making faces, sticking out their tongues and putting their thumbs in their ears and waving their fingers at people. It was so cute. All Roger and I could do was laugh. It is wonderful to be that age; one minute you try to act grown-up, and the next you are being silly. That is the way childhood should be.

We got to the Redbank club, and they were ready to get out. We had to help some of them straighten their clothes the girls were not used to wearing long dresses. Thank goodness, there was Linda. She would help to keep them in line and help repair any damage while they were standing in line, waiting to be introduced to the guest.

Then it was Roger and my turn and again to be called Mr. and Mrs. Roger Matthews Hilton. I waited a long time to be called that. I think I flushed every time someone said it. We went in, and we had the speeches. First, Jeremy introduced himself, but I'm sure everybody knew who he was. They had seen pictures of him, and they all knew he was his father's best man. He gave a wonderful speech about the twist and turns of life and how we end up where we do. He had Roger and me misty-eyed. We will never be able to express the thankfulness we have in our hearts for the chance to know and love him.

Ken gave a speech too, and so like him, it was done with either song titles or lyrics. It was beautiful, and we loved it. He always knew how much music meant to us; it is like the air we breathe. We are full of music all the time.

Now it was our turn, so Roger thanked all our guest for coming and helping us celebrate this momentous time of our life. We were happy to see everyone. Roger turned and gave me the microphone so I could say something to all our guest. I told everyone there we wanted them to meet our new best friend. She not only raised our son; she gave him back to us so we could love him along with her and his family. I introduced Jeremy's mother Cindy to all our family and friends. We had her come up and stand with us so everyone would know who she was. All we could do was hug her and tell her thank-you from the bottom of our hearts.

We then did our bride and groom dance we danced to "At Last" by Etta James; we felt like that was very appropriate, and we both like that song. After I danced, Jeremy asked me to dance, and I was happy to dance with him. While we were dancing, he told me something that had happened to him in the restroom at the reception. He told me my brother Will was in the bathroom at the same time and that Will had dropped a $100 bill, so Jeremy picked it up and handed it to him saying, "You dropped this." Will was very thankful he was giving the money to his youngest daughter so she could fly home the next morning because she had to go back to work.

After he told me the story, he asked me was that a test do you think to see if I was an honest man. I assured him we are not that type of people; we will assume you are who and what you say you are until you show us differently. He let out a sigh of relief, and we continued to dance.

Roger was dancing with Sara while I danced with Jeremy. I knew we were going to have to get ready to go through the food line because the food was ready, and we had delayed long enough.

When the music stopped, and we walked toward Roger and Sara, I told Roger, "We need to get these people fed now."

He said, "Yes, I know, so we checked with the caterers, and they were ready, so we told the bridal table that was on the stage to get ready to get in line behind us; we would start with the food. I asked Allen to announce that after the bridal table have gotten their food; it was time for everyone to eat. Roger and I fixed our plates, and then the rest of them followed.

Roger and I put our food on the table so we could go outside and run an errand. I am a diabetic and have to take a shot before I can eat, and Roger has to help me with my dress so he can put the shot in my thigh. We started outside, and Roger's brother Mark decided to tag along. I figured he would stop when we got to the end of the sidewalk, but he did not; he kept coming. I was squeezing Roger's hand so he knew I was not happy; we did not need an audience for this. Finally, Roger stopped and told Mark he needed to go back because he needed a moment of privacy, so I could take my shot.

Mark said, "Sorry, I will see you inside." We continued to the car and got it taken care off, but not without a lot of laughter, with me trying to hold my dress out of the way and him trying to put the shot in my thigh with my dress getting in the way. We got there, and we were walking back inside when I saw my brother Kline outside, smoking. I did not say anything, but I knew he saw us.

We went back to our table and explained to the children where we had been, and then we were able to eat; the food was so good, and we were hungry. While we were eating, the music was nice and mellow, and when we stopped eating and rose from the table, it was time to dance. My family dances; we always have we have music in our souls. My mother loved music too, and my father loved to dance. Roger and I started the dancing again, and then made our way around the room to thank everyone for coming and to take some pictures. Then my brother Kline came and got me and said, "Let's dance." I said, "Okay." I could see the twinkle in his eye. We no more got started dancing when he said, "You two could not wait. I saw you got to the parking lot?"

I was laughing. I said to him. "No, I had to have a shot before I ate."

He replied with "What kind of shot?"

Laughing, I said, "No, the shot for my diabetes before I eat."

He was laughing now too. I said, "Remember how old I am. I'm fifty-nine years old. I don't need anyone to take care of me." But he was having a good laugh.

Roger came and claimed his new bride and I told him, and he had to laugh too. Remarking forty-three years ago that is why he had to leave town. We looked at each other and smiled because we now belong to each other.

The dancing continued until it was time for the champagne and the cake-cutting. Our cake was beautiful. Tammy Karst made our wedding cake; it was three layers of lemon, carrot, and red velvet. She made the groom's cake too. Roger did not know he was getting a cake too; it was a surprise. It was a guitar-shaped cake, and it was marbled cake. They both tasted amazingly good. Tammy is Allen, our DJ's wife; he is Karl's son. So he is a nephew too. They very graciously help us with this reception.

It was getting late, and we were seeing people get ready to go, and we had more pictures to take.

Some of Roger and his siblings and me and mine. I am glad we got the ones we did of Rogers' family; they don't get together every year like my family does. They all talk, but they live in different places, so it makes it harder. Four of my siblings live in the Charleston Area, and I did too until this evening. Now I will live in Maine.

After almost everyone left, we still had things to do. We had to pay for any remaining things on the reception and get the basket of food the caters had packed for us and anything anyone might have forgotten, and all the wedding presents had to be put in our car. Lori and her family helped us do that, after Roger brought the car around to the front of the building. I did not help them do that. I was in a predicament, I had taken my shoes off when I was dancing, and when I went to put them on, they would not go on my feet. My feet were swollen, and my shoes had given me blisters. I could not wear them. There was a shallow trash bin close to where I was sitting, so I dropped them in there and told the girls working there it they wanted them to help themselves. They were expensive shoes, but they were not going on my feet again. When we were done, Roger helped me to the car while a waitress brought our food basket and wished us a happy life together.

We went to Bonnie's. I needed a pair of slippers to wear until I could get to my clothes and shoes. They were already at the rondel at Short Stay. I had only kept the clothes I needed to wear today at the church and then my wedding attire. What a surprise we got. When we got there, all but one of my siblings were there. They came to eat wedding cake and drink coffee. It was nice to see them again when we swept in with all our wedding regalia still on. Roger went in and just became one of the guys like always and all the girls were commiserating over my feet. Bonnie got me a pair of her slippers to wear to the lake, so we had cake and coffee too.

Shortly thereafter, we left them to it and went to the lake about a forty-minute drive. By the time we got there, we were exhausted and needed to change clothes before we did anything else. We each changed our clothes, and then we had to get the food and some things out of the car. After we did that and we were inside and safe, I told Roger I was going to take a shower and get ready for bed. He told me he would get things sorted for the morning. We had a 9:00 a.m. appointment downtown to tell Jeremy, Sara, and the girls, Jeremy's mom Cindy and her husband Chris and Sara's parents and sister goodbye. We were going straight to Maine and would not see them for a while.

We got into bed, and I was in his arms, and we were both so tired and sleepy. We tried to talk, but we both fell asleep. That is what happens when you get married when you are old. You are so tired after the wedding hustle bustle; you just need to sleep. Then we had to get up early and go downtown. It was worth it, though. We went to "High Cotton" for breakfast, and it was extremely nice. Jeremy sat with us before breakfast while we were waiting to be seated and told us another encounter he had last night at the reception.

He said, "I was standing at the bar and this young lady said to me, 'I know who you are, so I will tell you who I am. I'm your cousin Ashley. My dad is Ken, Aunt Betty's youngest brother.' So I asked her, 'How do you keep track of this big family?' She laughed and said, 'Hey, there are people here that are kin to me, and I don't know them. They came out of the woodwork for this wedding.'"

"Well, they did," I replied and that is not all of them if I had invited all of them. We would have had to have a place three times as big as it was, and we did not want to overrun Roger's family, so we kept it to the minimum. Roger and I laughed about it going back to Goose Creek after we saw them off. We went to Bonnie's so I could return her slippers and spend some time with her. We spent a lot of time together, and I was going to miss being with her when I got to Maine.

When we finally got back to the lake after doing a bit of shopping so we could eat without going out, we were back to working; we had to unload the wedding presents and rearrange the car to get all my clothes in there and repack our wedding finery. We open some of the gifts and then put them all together so we could put them in the trailer we had on hold to rent to carry my things to Maine.

Chapter 26

The next morning, we were up and running; we went and got the trailer and Lori and some friends helped us load it at the storage facility. After we loaded the trailer, we realized there was something wrong with the lights, so we went back to the rental company, and they had to issue us a new trailer; what did we do to deserve this?

I called Lori; she and her friends and helped us unload one trailer and put the stuff in the other one. Boy, were we glad to be done; now it was time to tell everyone goodbye. We were leaving first thing the next morning, and like the other times, I did not know when I would be back. It was the best of times and the worst of times. I had lived in and around Goose Creek for the last fifty-nine years with the exception of seven months where we had lived in Black Mountain, North Carolina. So I was sad to leave my children, grandchildren, and siblings and friends, and not know when I would see them again was gut-wrenching to say the least. But I was going with Roger to live with him as man and wife; that thought made me the happiest woman in the world, and I know this is what GOD wants me to do.

The drive to Maine was fine; we made good time. We needed to so Roger could go back to work. When we got home, we brought in the stuff we needed right away and waited till the next day to unload. One day would not make that much difference in the cost. We were again tired and needed to rest. We ate a potpie for dinner, and I went upstairs to take a shower and get ready for bed. Roger was not far behind me. My things that I left there were in the guestroom, so I did not need much that night. When we laid down, we talked about our trip and the wedding once again. We were beat. Roger pulled me close and said, "Now you are all mine." I knew what he meant; until we were married and back in Maine other people had dibs on our time. Now we are alone and going to stay that way.

We unloaded the trailer, and I moved my things from the guestroom into the master suite. The guestroom was no longer my place. It was open for guest. Now that room was going to be occupied with our suitcases so we could pack for our honeymoon. Lots to do and a month and a half to get ready. We were going to fly from Maine to New York and then to Barcelona, Spain. That is where we will board the ship for our cruise. I was extremely excited and scared to death too. I am scared of water. I did learn to swim in a pool after Cleo almost drowned when he was five years old at a family reunion by the river, and that was the last time we went there for a reunion.

Roger very politely told me if anything happened, he would save me, and I believe him. He was in the navy and a sailor for thirty years, but he served his time on a plane, not on a boat. I felt sure I would be fine. I believed in him; that is what wives do, right? Instead of worrying about it, I spent my time getting things ready. I had to add a few things that I needed and some he needed too.

In a truly short period of time, we were in a routine, and things were humming along fine. Roger went to work four days a week, and the other three days, we shopped and played. The scenery in Maine is gorgeous, and in some places, it is breathtaking, and he always had a new place he wanted to show me, and I was happy to go along.

Packing for the Mediterranean was different. I thought it would be very warm like it is in South Carolina in late April and early May. Roger told me that it would be warm when we went to North Africa, but on the northern side of the Mediterranean, it would be cooler because it is about ten times more north from the equator than Charleston, South Carolina. It was capri pants for the daytime and slacks and dresses for the nighttime and a sweater or wrap close to hand. After worrying about that we needed to concentrate on our medication, making sure we had enough to get us back home with some leftover for emergencies. After that, we needed haircuts before we left too.

In no time at all, we were ready to go and so happy to be going; he had set everything up so we would be taken care of, and I could hardly wait. We ordered a taxi to take us to the airport and then we were off. It was going to be a dream come true; something every girl wants her husband to do for her.

We had a short trip to LaGuardia Airport in New York and then a very long flight to Barcelona, Spain. I was so weary, but we stayed up and spent the day sightseeing. We had tapas to eat, but the best thing was going to the Gaudi Familia Church in Barcelona or the Basilica de la Sagrada also known as the Sagrada Familia. They started building this Catholic Church in 1882. The original architect was Antoni Gaudi. This church is breathtaking; the whole church is huge and very grand. The columns inside the church look like tree trunks. The windows look like honeycombs. It is all taken from nature on the inside. Only two sides are finished on the outside the back and front the back is all about the Nativity. There is a scene of the birth of Jesus, the wise men, the shepherds, and the soldiers killing the babies when looking for Jesus. The front side is done in modern art; it is gorgeous too. There is the Crucifixion, the Last Supper, Peter with the cock that crowed three times, and lots more. You just can't stop looking at it always searching for other clues. After spending hours at the church, we had dinner and went to bed early we were exhausted. Did I say weddings were exhausting? Well, so are honeymoons! The next morning, we were ready to go to our ship when we went outside. We found other people that had stayed on our hotel that were going on the cruise with us. The booking company had everything done for us; our transportation was arranged. We only had to get in line to go to the ship.

Before we knew it, we turned in our luggage and we were on the ship. I have never been on a cruise. I always remember reading about the *Titanic* and *The Lusitania* but Roger promised we would be okay; besides there is a Higher Power I put my faith in and everybody that knows me knows that is how I feel. We walked around the ship before going to our room, then there was someone there to show us where to go. We were in the middle of the ship as requested. Not far from the elevator.

Roger told me we were going to have a nice room, but my goodness it was fabulous; when we went, it was a whole wall of windows.

It was gorgeous and so high up. I had not expected such grandeur. We had everything a huge bed and sitting room set, a dressing room with a vanity and a nice glassed-in tub and shower in a separate room. As we looked at everything, the steward introduced himself and told us he and his partner would be taking care of us. Then he said there is a concierge's room a few doors down past the elevator, and there are always drinks and snacks when we needed them. If we were hungry after dinner and needed a bedtime snack, just call and they would bring it to us. Such luxury this girl had never experienced before. Oh, then we walk out on to the balcony. My word! It was as long as our room with chairs and a table. I was leaning on the rail when Roger came up behind me and wrapped me in his arms and asked, "Do you like it?"

I was like, "What is not to like I feel like a queen."

"That is wonderful. That is what I was shooting for." I turned in his arms and kissed him. He is always thinking what it is I would like nobody could ask for better or find a better husband. We went looking for something to eat and found the buffets and not a lot of people yet, so we had lunch and went walking around, checking things out, finding our way around, so we would know where things were. We went back to our room to find our luggage there, so we unpacked and put our clothes away. The boat was leaving port so we went out on the deck so we could see what was happening. I was amazed at how they move these big vessels; they just back them up and go. It looked awesome to me then; we were on the water and sailing. It was magnificent, the breeze, the sky, all of it; as you can guess, I have never been on a boat in the past. I have always been afraid of water.

We freshened up and was getting ready to go out again. There was a knock on the door. It was our stewards; they had come to collect our empty luggage and to tell us what to expect they would turn down our bed while we were at dinner, collect our dirty laundry in the morning, and now they would show us were the concierge was. So off we went to, and it was lovely; they had drinks of all kinds, petit fours, hors d'oeuvres, small sandwiches, and cheese trays. Other people in there were having a snack and cocktails. We had soft drinks and a snack; then we left to walk around and to later to find some dinner.

We are heading for the Port of Tunis, Tunisia, so we were going to have a long day the next day, and we needed to get some rest from our jetlag. We are going to see the roman baths, and we are going to Carthage and some museums. I was so tired. I knew I would sleep even though I was on a ship because you could hardly tell we were moving unless you were outside. We went out briefly to see the stars, and it was gorgeous. We were up and looking for breakfast early, so we would be ready to go on time. This was a visit I did not want to miss. I had read about these places all my life, and I am going there now. Woohoo! We got on shore, and it was hot and the white houses with the blue roofs and shutters looked like a picture post card.

We were the first boat to come ashore in a long time; the first place we went was through the market. Now that was different. Everyone wanted to sell you something. We stayed around a while and looked at things then we had to leave to go Carthage. I had read about Carthage a lot in history books, and I read that the Romans salted the land before they left, but they did not.

It was interesting, and the museum was wonderful. We spent quite a while in there looking at the objects from long ago. What people do not seem to understand is that they made things to use in everyday life just like we do. Sometimes, these are the most significant pieces of our history. We also went to the Roman baths, and they were quite beautiful. The colors were bright and bold, and we got to see how they function and how the water was supplied. The people lounging in the pools were fine, but the workers had hard intense hot work to do. It has been like that from the beginning of time, the haves and the have nots. Finally, it was time to go back to the boat, but not before the camel owners tried to get you to take a ride. They are called the ships of the desert because you sway when you ride them, but that was not for me getting past the smell was enough. Phew. Another night and another destination the next day. Roger found us a nice restaurant to have dinner at that night, and we walked around all the venues of the ship, seeing as much as we could. Leaving some for another night and planning to see some shows.

We are now in Trapani, Sicily; it is raining and cold. We had no idea how cold it would be. Just across the Mediterranean Sea, there we saw an Athenian temple that was truly majestic and beautiful. Until you see them, you have no idea of the scale of these things. The columns are tremendous in size. Everything about them is huge, then we went to an amphitheater carved out of a mountain long time ago. The things they did in these places were mind-blowing when you think about the tools they had to work with. We were all glad to get back on the ship that day; although I was not as bad off as some. My new husband gave me his jacket to wear and kept his arms around me, and we did better than most. Chivalry is not dead.

Chapter 27

When the ship was getting ready to leave. We were getting dressed to meet the captain of the ship and go to dinner. We were all dressed up because of dinner, and we were having our honeymoon pictures made later in the evening. The captain who was a Norwegian asked Roger, "With you being in the US Navy for thirty years, I guess you spent a lot of time at sea?"

Roger laughed and told him, "This is the longest I have ever been on a ship. The only time I spent on a ship was when we had long missions and had to bingo aboard for fuel. No, I flew with the navy all those years. I was an Electronics Intelligence Operator Air Crew Member." So now they were swapping stories about the navy, so I looked around and let them talk. After dinner, we walked around the outside of the ship until it was time for our appointment to have our pictures taken; it was a magical, wonderful evening.

I am going to Rome, Italy. I can hardly wait. I have read so much about it, and now I am going.

The ship pulled into our port of call, which is Civitavecchia. We were again up and had breakfast and ready for the day, which was going to be a long one. We were about fifty miles from Rome, and we were going to see as much as we could. Roger has been here before; he even went to see the pope years before. Now it is my turn to see everything I can. The bus ride was nice, and Roger and I talked about what we were going to see. He tried to make me understand how big everything was going to be, like the temple we saw in Sicily, I told him, "I understand. I have been to Washington, DC, where buildings are as big as city blocks."

He smiled and said, "These things are bigger than the temple we saw in Sicily." I just looked at him while he smiled.

We stopped and had lunch before going all the way into the city; the first thing that caught my eye was the policemen on the street with what looked like machine guns or AK47s. I don't know what they are called but had never seen them on the street before. I told Roger, "Look at the gun the police are carrying. Is something going on?"

And he assured me, "Everything was fine. That is normal for Italy."

"But why?" was my question.

He said, "They have a lot of kidnappings in in big cities like Rome." I could hardly wrap my head around it; the people seemed to be fine. I did not see any reactions; I thought it was just odd. Another thing they are absolutely the worst drivers I have ever seen. We were in the middle of things now. I did not know where to look first; it was awesomely big everything was huge. We went to the Trevi Fountain. It was the day they clean the fountain. I was sad I wanted to throw a coin in the fountain, and they were sweeping up the money.

Roger said, "Look, there is a gelato shop. Let's go get some you will like it." We waited in line, and when we came out, the fountain was back on; he laughed at me, just like I was a child, but I really was glad, and I threw my coin in the fountain. That is supposed to mean I will come back to Rome. I know it is true. I saw it in a movie and read it in a book. I am smiling as I write this.

Then we were off to the Colosseum built in 70–80 AD. What an amazing sight it is, monstrous, and to think they built that all those years ago. Roger was filming me with the video camera while I was looking at it. I told him, "I would stay outside even though you could not go in because I'm a Christian, and I knew what happened to Christians in there."

He said, "Yes, but that was a long time ago."

I told him it did not matter; those people died because they loved my JESUS. We went it the Arch of Titus; he destroyed Jerusalem in 70 AD, and the Israelites were not allowed to come back to the city. The only thing good about the arch is he recorded the Menorah and other Israeli things he took from there so the people of God have a record of how things looked.

When we left there, we went to the Vatican. I had seen pictures of the pope and inside of the Vatican; however, I did not know it had a thirty-six feet wall around it, that is around ten feet thick. Our guide is wonderful. When we went into the Holy See, she took us to a map on a wall to see where everything was. She knew her history and her way around the place. She answered all our questions and took us to the places we wanted to go, then we went by ourselves to see as much as we could. Like the Sistine Chapel, the chapel is unbelievable; they were cleaning it and the grandeur of the colors from that long ago is breathtaking. We walked through the museum and saw the gifts that had been given to the church by the leaders of the world's countries. Some were amazing and some not so much, depending on who was president or the monarchs of said nations. What I found extraordinary was the pieces of art they had sent the great artist like Michelangelo out in the world to collect from other nations and lands. The artwork was magnificent. I am glad it is open to the world to see. We did not go to St. Peter's Basilica because they were getting it ready for Pope John Paul's beatification. We stayed and saw as much as we could for the time we had. Then it was back to the bus and on our way to the ship for our next port of call the next day, which will be Portofino, the Italian Riviera.

Since the first night, we have not been to dinner at the buffet; that is all we knew about till the next day, then Roger discovered all the restaurants on board, and we have been trying them all out. Every night has been an adventure too. We are going to a swanky place tonight like all the other nights. My new husband has a thing about fine dining. Good thing I brought lots of dressy outfits that mix and match. We have been all over the boat to the shows, to the casino were Roger handed me twenty dollars and said, "Have fun." I played the slot machine for fun, and when I won my money back plus his twenty, I stopped. I do not like gambling; it gets people in trouble.

The next morning, we were excited to see the Italian Riviera. We were ready to go. We rode the boat ashore and started our day of rambling after wondering how people own yachts as big as military ships. They were huge stories above the little boats we were on. I was not impressed, though I do not like the water that much; the cruise ship has been wonderful, but that is the only kind of boat I want to be on. We got a soft drink at the dock and wandered around the shops. The prices of the things there were outrageous. I always look at things and see what they are, how they are made, and calculate in my head how much it would cost me to make it; that pretty much turns me off, expensive things.

I will tell you what it's like; my best friend wanted to cover two chairs she had in her bedroom so she could put them in the living room of her new house, so she got some estimates. They were astronomical, from four to eight hundred dollars. I told her we can do better that that. We went to a fabric warehouse, and she found the perfect fabric, cheap, and told me, "We need this much fabric to cover the chairs." I asked her, "Who said that?"

She told me, "The people I got the estimates from." I had measured her chairs, so I knew how much I needed to make the chairs and make the piping for the chairs and cushions. Two Queen Ann chairs, four yards of fabric, thread, and piping the size we needed. I covered her chairs, and when she moved into her new house, the men that brought her new sofa and love seat asked her about her lovely chairs. So she told them that her friend had covered them for her, and they wanted to know if I would like a job at their store. The guy was the assistant manager, the son of the owner. She told them she would ask. I told her, "No, thank you." Oh, I almost forgot it cost her around forty-five dollars for me to cover her chairs. I am not cheap, just frugal; if it's not on sale, I don't buy it unless it is an emergency.

Now back to the Italian Riviera. One shop had a crazy name. It was "Shabby Sheep." I guess they thought it was a fun name. They sold Rolex watches and other things there. After looking at the shops, we decided to climb the hill to see the Church of St. George. It was a long climb but gradual, and the church was interesting old church, very plain, but nice and appropriate. Now let us talk about the views we saw. They were astonishing. Looking out on the Mediterranean Sea from the outlook, watching the dolphins play in the water is all that is good for the soul; it makes me relax and I take a deep breath and know GOD created this for our enjoyment and enjoy is what we did. We walked back down the hill, enjoying the views again, knowing we were on our way to the lifeboats that would take us back to the *Eurodam*, our ship. We had two nights left on the ship; next stop, Monte Carlo.

When we got back to the ship and had dinner, we went again out on our deck and watched as the ship sailed to our next stop. It is so lovely to stand at the rail in each other's arms and talk about our day. Then go in and order coffee or cocoa to end our evening. This union between us is just as special as it always was. I love him so much, and I know he loves me. He tells me all the time, and I dare not look at or say I want something because he wants to buy it for me. So I am careful what I say when shopping with him. He is too generous. I hope we will live a long time so we will have many more good times.

What do you say about Monte Carlo? We took a bus ride through it to go to Nice. Now we will have fun. We went to the market there. What could be better food, flowers, and beach? We ate and walked through the market; it is laid out in sections. Food, then the flowers: they are gorgeous; the colors are so vibrant, and luckily, Roger knew a lot about them. He spent years over here while he was in the navy, and he likes flowers, and I could admire them and find out what they were. Then we went to the beach, not into the water. We just walked around watching the people in the water and laying on the sand. I was astonished to see topless women out there. I know they do that, but it was a shock to see. I am an old prude, some would say, but that is the way it is. I am a grandmother, after all, who was raised in a Christian environment. It was hot so we went back to the flowers and goods market. We got back on the bus and went to an area where the ones that wanted to could climb this mountain to see a castle. I talked it over with Roger, and we decided to go to a coffee shop with Wi-Fi and get caught up with our families back home. We climbed enough the day before. After they got back, we boarded the bus to ride back to the ship, and an interesting ride it was too. We were going downhill, and you almost had to hold your breath.

This was to be our last night on the ship, so we dressed up and went for dinner. It was lovely, then we walked around on deck with other people but stayed to ourselves. We enjoyed just being together, watching the water and the waves and him keeping me warm. It was a nice way on which to end our honeymoon. I think we did very well being with so many other people.

We got back to the room so we could finish packing because they were going to pick up our luggage early, and I like everything in its proper place, and my clothes planned for the next day.

We knew it was going to be a long trip home.

The next morning, we put our luggage out so it could be collected and went to find coffee and breakfast. We did not linger. We had to be on the bus to the airport. The airport—UGH! When we got to the airport and got in this really long line to check in, we waited and waited. When we got to the counter, the nice young lady said to Roger, "That will be $150 for your extra luggage" and proceeded to tell him that they raised the price while we were on the ship from $50 to $75 each. So I asked why we were not told in advance. She did the wrong thing; she shrugged her shoulders at me like no skin off my nose. I then proceeded to tell her I wanted to see a manager, and if not, I would open that suitcase and put all this clothes on here in front of her and everybody and that suitcase contained my PJs and my underclothes. She called a manager.

We were escorted to the desk in the back, and Roger just let me roll after he rolled his eyes at me. I told the manager it was highway robbery, and no one had told us ahead of time this was going to happen, not them nor Delta, with whom we booked with. Then I told him these things do not happen overnight, and someone had better fix it. I think the young lady had told them what I said about my clothes because he said, "Yes, we can do that." So we paid our $100 and then we went to our next checkpoint, which was customs. We sailed through the rest of the time and then boarded the plane.

We got to Amsterdam on time and had a layover of four hours, but that was okay. We were going to gain about six hours coming across the Atlantic, as we were chasing the sun. The flight to Detroit was great. We were on a great big plane that was about 20 percent full. The flight attendants were wonderful; they came by and asked if we wanted anything, and we told them our story, and they wanted all the details. After we told them as much as we could, they brought us chocolate cake, cookies, and coffee. They also brought us two bottles of champagne to take home with us and told us if asked at customs where it came from tell them it was an American plane we were on.

We landed in Detroit and the airport was closed, and it was closing. Ours was the last plane to land that night. They hurried us through customs with me holding two bottles of champagne in a grocery bag. I was asked if we had anything to declare, and I told them no because we did not have anything to declare. We went straight to board our plane, and we were off to Portland, and then a thirty-minute drive in a taxi to Brunswick, Maine, home.

We were glad to be home and sleep in our own bed; it was a wonderful honeymoon, but now, we are back to reality. Life would go back to normal, and there were things we needed to do. Wesley, Nathan, and Chelsea were coming to stay a month when school was finished for the year, and I could hardly wait to see my babies.

Chapter 28

They would not like me to call them my babies; they do not think of themselves as babies, but when you are the grandmother and you helped raise them, they are your babies. I will fly to Myrtle Beach, South Carolina, and one of the parents, Cleo or Lori, will bring them to meet me at the airport and then we will fly back to Maine. It is now May, and they will be coming in the second week of June for three or four weeks. I am getting the rooms situated so they will be ready for them, other than the master suite we have two other rooms upstairs and an office, and we have a basement that has a small kitchen, bath, a TV room, bedroom, and a workshop. They will have plenty of places to stay. Wesley is thirteen years old, Nathan is nine years old, and Chelsea is twelve years old. They are really good children. I used to take them everywhere. Wesley has lived with me since he was born apart from when he lived in Florida for six months with his mother and another six months here in an apartment and the summer visits with his dad. Nathan has lived with me since he was born apart from six months his mother lived in an apartment. I love these children so much; they made my life happy, and I, in turn, raised them in the church and taught them to be good human beings and to love JESUS. Some parents don't know it, but GOD will hold you accountable for not teaching your children about HIM.

I think Roger is wondering what it will be like to have grandchildren in the house; he raised other people's eighteen- to twenty-two-year-olds in the US Navy. These kids play hard eat good and hog the TV, but that's okay with me.

We have been doing some exploring; well, Roger has been taking me to places I have never been, and it is so beautiful here. There are all kind of places we can go to. It's still May here, and it is still cold, but I like it. Living in South Carolina was way too hot for me. Usually down there in May, it is hot and sticky, and it only gets worse as summer comes. Up here in Maine, it is in the sixties during the day and cold at night.

The grands will be coming before I know it, I am going grocery shopping so I can fix their favorite foods and desserts, like baked macaroni and cheese, chicken alfredo with broccoli, and chocolate pie. I sure wish our other granddaughters were going to be here so they could all spend some time together, and I could love on them too. We have met a couple of times, and I know their parents are not ready to let them loose. Oh well, maybe they will bring them up here next year.

Roger and I are happy every day because it is a new day to love each other; the love we have just pours out of us both. We were shopping the other day, and we told the lady helping us our story and she told us, "The love shines out of your eyes, and you glow." What a nice compliment. We are so thankful to be together and thank GOD every night and day that we are.

Everything is ready, and it is time for me to fly to Myrtle Beach. I am starting early to fly down, and it will be a long day, but a happy one for me. Roger is driving me to the airport and will pick us up when we get back. As soon as I get used to driving here, I can do it myself; for now, he will.

I was reading while I was on the plane when I was not missing Roger. Last time on the plane we were on our honeymoon. I was so excited to get off the plane. I was glad I had no luggage to worry about. I was hunting for my children, and I soon found them, and they saw me and came running. I cannot tell you how wonderful it is. There was hugs and kisses all around. I told the boys to tell Uncle Cleo thank you for bringing them to the airport from Goose Creek and told Chelsea to hug and kiss her daddy bye; we have a plane to catch. I kissed Cleo bye too, and we were off.

Nathan was sitting by me, and I let Wesley and Chelsea sit across from me. I was keeping an eye on them, and I knew where Nathan wanted to sit, not far from Mama. It was only a couple of hours, and they were good and knew how to behave. They enjoyed getting a snack and drink from the flight attendant, even though I gotten them some snacks at the airport before we left. This was the first time the boys had been in an airplane; it was all new to them and they wanted to look out the windows.

Before we knew it, we were landing in Portland; we had to round up their luggage and go meet Grandpa. He was there as I knew he would be, and they were glad to see him. Each one took a turn hugging him. Then it was Grandpa this and Grandpa that all about the flight there. He just listened and smiled at them, but he did answer their questions too; they knew he flew a long time in the navy and that he is a pilot too. The first thing we did was take them to get something to eat; children in general like to eat out regularly, and these children love eating out so that is what we did. We let them choose, and they chose Denny's. I knew they would as soon as I saw it; they are predictable where food is concerned.

We got home in good time after feeding them, I was waiting to see what they thought about Grandpa's and my house; it came as soon as Grandpa was not in the room. "Mama, is Grandpa rich? This is such a big house." I had to laugh it is a big house my house where they grew up would have fit into part of one floor in this house. They wanted to see the rest, and the first thing they found when we went exploring was the chairlift on the stairs. I let each have a turn and then that was done. I told them it was not a toy they said, "Yes, ma'am."

Chelsea wanted the guest room I stayed in when I was visiting before we were married, so that let one other available room upstairs with a twin bed in it. Nathan said, "This is mine, and Mama, where is your room?" I showed them my room and then Wesley said, "Where am I sleeping?" We were off again to go to the basement to show Wesley another bedroom and was he happy, he told the other two, "You stay up upstairs. This is mine." A TV room, bedroom, and a bathroom all by myself. That is when the arguing started. At first, I told them, "You chose your room, and this is all that is left for Wesley." Then I told Wesley, "You have to share the TV with them because I am not watching your shows." That satisfied them all.

We spent the next couple of weeks on the go, taking them to see the lighthouse in Portland; we took them to the beach at Old Orchard Beach, and just like me; we had never seen a beach without sand. The beaches in Maine have little tiny pebbles on their beaches. They are brave kids. They went into the water and played, and when they came out of the water, they were turning blue; there is no nice bathwater temperatures in the ocean here like in Charleston, South Carolina.

We planned most of the outings when Grandpa was off work on his long weekends. We took them to a water park somewhere and we all played Putt-Putt, walked around, and had fun then the saw this super slide they wanted to ride so we let them, and they said, "Grandpa, take Mama for a ride on it" and he said OKAY. I had to walk up SEVEN flights of stairs to get to the top and then got into a round raft to slide down on this contraption, and when we did and stopped at the bottom, Roger was sitting on my head. The children loved it.

Our next destination was Camden, Maine. We rode a long way so they could see more of Maine, and they were good sports about it. We toured the usual spots fed them a nice lunch did some shopping and went back home everyone had fun.

During the week, I took them shopping too for things they wanted and for things they needed. They also went grocery shopping with me; they liked to pick out their favorite foods and snacks to eat, so I let them. I did not know when I was going to see them again, so I spoiled them with things I could not always buy for them. They knew when we lived together I had just so much money for groceries and did not ask for a lot, so now I let them get what they wanted. After all, they helped Grandpa and me cut the grass. Wesley did okay. Chelsea, not so much; she cut one of the Hostas in half. She was so upset, but Grandpa hugged her and told her, "It is just a plant after all, no big deal." That made her feel better, and now she loved him too. I could see it in her eyes.

Before it was time for them to go back home, we took them to Boston; we drove to Portland and got a train to Boston. That was something else they had never done road in a train. If that was not cool enough, we got tickets for the duck boat. They loved that, and my Nathan got to drive the duck boat; he was impressed with himself. He is too cute.

Now it was time for them to go back home. I knew I would miss them, but Mama is too old to be raising children, and I like being just Mama, not the disciplinarian in their lives. I thank GOD every day for them. They filled the twelve and a half years I was a widow with love and fun and happiness. I flew back to Myrtle Beach with them. Lori was there to meet us and take them home, but because our plane was late, I spent the day there until a later flight that evening. When I finally got back to Portland, I was so tired I could have cried, but I did not because my wonderful husband was there waiting for me. We were back on our own and ready to be on our own. I love those children, but they do make me tired. But that is okay. I'll see them as soon as possible!

Chapter 29

Roger was back at work, and I was keeping house and cooking. I enjoy that, and he likes to eat. I fix us breakfast, and while cleaning the kitchen after breakfast, I start making dinner so he will have a hot meal to take to work with him. We are back on our routine, and things are back to normal until I got a phone call from Evelyn and Bonnie telling me Lori was in the hospital. She has plaque psoriasis on her ankles, and she scratched it, and it is now infected. She has cellulitis, and they gave her some medicine for that, and it shut down her kidneys; now she has to have dialysis. The reason Evelyn and Bonnie called me is because Evelyn is a dialysis nurse.

That is what she does at work; she wanted to impress upon me just what was happening. I told her I would be there the next day. Roger got me a plane ticket and rented me a car and then took me to the airport. This is what mothers do when their children need them. I went straight to the hospital to see Lori; her foot looked like it had a semiclear golf ball on top of her foot right below her forth and little toe. These are the times when you cannot be in two places at one time. I stayed until she was ready to go home and spent some time with the boys between the times I was at the hospital.

I got back home and just kept in touch with her. I talk to her most days and the boys when they are around. Roger met me at the airport; he was glad to have me back. Well, he said he was. We are always ready for whatever is next, not knowing what is going on drives me crazy, so I am trying to let my grown children live their own lives. Let me tell you, it is not easy, for so many years, they were under my feet and so were their children, and now it like sometimes they are saying, "Mama who?" But I just give it to the Lord and close my eyes and go to sleep until something goes wrong, then I need hands on, and sometimes I need face-to-face.

We talk to Jeremy and Sara more now and keep up with what the girls are doing. The girls are both playing soccer and loving it; we went down there for a couple of days in the fall to visit and enjoyed spending time with them all. Ana and Sophie are just little dolls; they are funny, cute, and smart as can be. They can hold their own in a restaurant they know what to order and how to order and always with a please and thank-you. I will tell you watching Roger with them almost makes me want to weep. He is finding it all so new, and they could probably ask for the moon and he would try to get it for them. They do not know it yet, but they have his heart in the palms of their little hands. That is not to say he does not feel the same about Jeremy and Sara his face lights up when either one of them calls. He is such a good man, and he deserves this. I know in the beginning of our relationship, when we were teenagers and things took a bad turn and we did not get married, I was so disappointed and said some hurtful things about him, but in my heart, I never stopped loving him and I am overjoyed now that he has this chance to be a father and friend to Jeremy and Sara and a lovable grandpa to the girls. What we have gained is never far from the both of us; we talk about how blessed we are all the time.

Before we knew it, summer was over, and fall was upon us and here in Maine; it does not play around. The sun goes down early, the temperature drops and Halloween, Thanksgiving, and Christmas will be here shortly. I started early making list for the grands. I plan on mailing some things and the others we will let Amazon do the work. Jeremy and Sara will have to tell us what they want. I have some ideas for Cleo and Nikki. Lori and Henry will be pretty easy to shop for I have shopped for them since they got married and know what they like and want. As for the grandchildren, Krissy will get a gift card nobody knows what teenagers want then that leaves Wesley, Chelsea, Ana, Nathan, and Sophie. I'll find out from their parents what they would like, and I will get them all some clothes. Then I have to shop for Roger; this is a chore he orders whatever he wants or thinks he needs, and it shows up at the house. I think I will reign him in so some of the rest of us will have a chance to shop for him.

We got ready for Halloween my least favorite holiday day, but I like seeing the little children dress up and coming for candy. It is the amount of money, and the crazy things adults do that drive me crazy; it is just weird we would never spend great amounts of money to dress up one night and go to a party, not when you have children they always come first. Do not think I did not let my children and grands dress up. I did, and they had nice costumes because I made them.

Halloween was a relativity easy night; we live on a quiet street and had only a few children come by, so that was easy enough except for the leftover candy. Before the night was over, Roger and I were discussing Thanksgiving and my birthday, which would be on the same day this year. I am going to be sixty years old. I wonder some times where the years went and realize I have a heart full of memories of my children the two I raised and the one I yearned for. It makes me say "Thank you, LORD, for all the blessings I have had and have now."

I told Roger I was going to cook Thanksgiving anyway even if it is my birthday, and then we decided to wait until the weekend so he would be home, and we could eat together. We celebrated my birthday on my birthday and waited for the weekend to cook that gave me time to make desserts. We invited Cheryl, Roger's stepdaughter, over too, and she came and brought a nice vegetable salad. The evening was pleasant, and we enjoyed the company, and we ate plenty. We also thanked GOD for the blessings that had been bestowed on us this pass year.

Christmas is different this year not being with my children, grandchildren, siblings, and friends back in South Carolina. I am happy where I am, but I miss them all. I used to go shopping with Sherry late at night in Walmart for the children, and we went down the toy aisles and played with all the toys. Bringing toys home and hiding them until Christmas. It was an adventure, but this year, I ordered it and had it delivered or mailed it to Lori already wrapped, for her to put under the tree from me and Grandpa. This is the first

Christmas I have ever spent away from my siblings, my children, and grandchildren, but everything is right in my world. I am exactly where I want to be and where GOD wants me to be.

It's Christmas morning and my wonderful husband does not have to work, we will have breakfast and talk to our families together and then celebrate Christmas together and then we are going across the street to Dr. John's and his lovely family home for Christmas dinner. We had a lovely time, and the food was scrumptious, and the family was delightful. We went home later with full stomachs thoroughly satisfied.

We talked to all our children and our siblings throughout the day, so all told it was a lovely Christmas. It was cold and had snow on the ground, and the air was clean and clear. A crisp winter night like we grew up imagining when we lived down south. It gets dark at like four o'clock in the afternoon, so we had a nice, long evening together. It makes you wonder about the night our LORD and SAVIOR was born so long ago.

Chapter 30

It is the New Year 2012 when we were kids dating; we never thought the world would last this long with the wars and nuclear weapons. We thought Jesus would have come by now to save us all. We are glad to be here; we have so much to live for the both of us, with each other and with our children, grandchildren, and families. Life is wonderful here in Maine; we are so happy together. We have work to do, though, things to fix and change in the house. We do not plan to stay in the Maine when Roger retires from LL Bean.

The first thing I have to do is get my rotator-cuff repaired, which involves surgery—ouch, but better to get it done now while it is cold. I would hate to wear a sling when it is hot. I hate being hot. I can always put clothes on and get warm, but when it is hot you are stuck. My surgery went okay, and the doctor gave me some pain medicine that he assured me would not give me hives, and an hour after I got home, I was back in the emergency room with hives and itching so bad I was going crazy. So now the only oral pain killer I can take is Tramadol, so for the next three months, until I healed and quite aching, I will wear an icepack on my shoulder.

So now the surgery is over, and the doctor told me no vacuuming, sweeping, or mopping. So you tell me how to do housework without doing those things. I did my therapy and got the use of my shoulder and a full range of movement back and that is good, but I need to do things Roger said not to vacuum we have a Roomba, but the Roomba is round, and we have square corners in this house. I think most houses do, so I have to dust or Swiffer the corners. Yes, I know I have OCD, but so did my mother and all my siblings. It will get better, I am sure; in the meantime, I will do it when he has gone to work.

In March, we celebrated our first anniversary. Roger took me to Bar Harbor Maine. We stayed at the Atlantic Oceanside Hotel and Conference Center. We had a wonderful time, even though it was cold and snow on the ground. He gave me a beautiful pair of drop pearl earrings for my anniversary. He also wined and dined me like he always does for special days. He spoils me, and I love him as far as the east is from the west.

After Jeremy's birthday in April, he called his father and asked him when he was going to retire. Roger told him in a year or so. Jeremy then asked him if we were going to stay in Maine, and Roger told him no we thought we would move south, that we needed a tax-friendly state and Jeremy told him Tennessee is a tax-friendly state. Roger told him he knew that, and we talked about Tennessee, Florida, and Texas. We had decided Texas and Florida were too hot for us, so we were looking to move to east Tennessee maybe by a lake. Jeremy told him that was great that he wanted us closer to them, and Roger told him we would come down in a week or two and buy a house.

When Roger told me, I was astonished. I knew we had talked about Tennessee, but buy a house in two weeks! Oh my goodness! It was really going to happen, and I would be closer to my other children too.

We flew to Tennessee, and Sara told us she would be our agent and that was awfully nice of her, and she has lived there all her life and knows where to look and where not to look. As it happened, when her parents knew we were coming they invited us to stay with them and not stay in a hotel.

We accepted their invitation; it was lovely to stay with them we had the upstairs all to ourselves. They have a big beautiful home and extremely comfortable. They are very gracious, and we are becoming exceptionally good friends. They are the same sort of people we are, hardworking, and loving our GOD, our families, and our country.

As it turned out, we looked at a lot of houses, and we saw some that we liked and some not so much, and then Dave told Sara about one in Oak Ridge that he saw in the paper so off we went to look at it, when I say we that means Dave and Marylee, Jeremy and Sara,

Ana and Sophie, our granddaughters, and Roger and myself. Well, let me tell you, like some things about it and some not at all and said as much to Roger. He said, "Okay, we will talk about it." I knew this was the house he wanted. Poor Roger when he bought the house we live in now, he had to promise to paint it and have a tree taken out of the front yard so Irene his first wife would agree to move there. I knew he was willing to compromise with me about this house. We came to an agreement about what I wanted to change. I told him I wanted him to take Jeremy aside and ask him if this house was too close to them and his in-laws, and he told Roger no this is where I want you to be. That was all we had to hear we bought the house.

We did all the paperwork before we went back to Maine and closed from there. We came down one more time after closing to measure the rooms and map everything out so we would know how much furniture to bring back when we moved. Then we gave Jeremy the keys so he could lease it, and he did right away to a young family for one year because we were coming back the next September or October.

We had things to do and started focusing on what we wanted to do to the house before we put it on the market; we had a year to do it, and I just made some list and we bought things we needed, and I did have a break. I went back to Myrtle Beach to get the boys Chelsea could not come for a summer visit, and I was sorry she was not there. We did fun things with them while they were there, and they helped us do some work outside too; always love having my boys with me. They are good sports about helping me do things and when they get trifling. I am not above putting my foot down or bribing them. Hey, it is what grandmothers do.

August came, and we were so excited. Jeremy, Sara, Ana, and Sophie came for a week. We rented a van so we could all travel around and have room for everyone. Sara and the girls arrived a few days before Jeremy; he was working but coming right away. We were so glad to see them it was in May when we saw them last while we were down there purchasing the house in Oak Ridge, Tennessee. They had never been to Maine, and we had lots of places to take them. The day after they arrived, we took them to Old Orchard Beach. The water was freezing but the girls went in to swim just like my other grandchildren they turned blue. But the funniest thing that happened all day was when we told Sara it was about a forty-five-minute to an hour drive; she was like "Okay." In Maine, things are not close together and the rides are sometime long, so she went to sleep when we pull into the beach parking lot, the guy said that will be ten dollars and the sleeping Sara said pulling money out of her purse said, "I have ten dollars." Then she told Roger, "I am ready to be done with this ride. All your rides take forever." We enjoyed our day out and the girls enjoyed their day at the beach. I stuck my feet in the cold water; that was enough for me.

We talked to Jeremy the next day, and it was decided we would meet him in Bangor the next day; from there, we are going to Bar Harbor we are going whale and puffin watching. We picked Jeremy up and then we went shopping at the LL Bean store up there. Jeremy needed a few things and so did Roger. That done, it was time to go eat, Jeremy, Sara, and Roger had lobster dinner. Me, I had fish and the girls had lobster too they are carnivores, usually just meat and bread. That is strange for a person like me. I mostly eat vegetables. We went back to our hotel, The Bar Harbor Grand Hotel. We had been traveling all day, and we were tired.

The next day, we went to the whale watching ship very early, and there were lots of people waiting to get on, that's when the ship company decided they needed to take two ships, so we waited for the next one as this one was full. The new ship was a delight to be on; it was a ship built for about four hundred people, and there we only about 150 people on it so we could move around get coffee and watch everything. After we got away from the shore, everyone was excited to see a puffin, and then we were watching for whales.

They are magnificent creatures; the biologist on board told us all about them and what their names were. A little later, I was watching Ana. She was standing along the rail on the inside of the catamaran when one of the whales decided it wanted a better look at us and came up between the two hulls of the boat. I could not believe it was right there and big as can be and she could hardly believe it either. Trust me when I say the boat captain and the biologist were scared too, you could hear the quiver in the voice of the biologist as she told us to just be still that the captain was going to back us away from the whale very slowly. It would not get hurt; we did not have a propeller on our boat. What a beautiful and breathtaking trip. It was late afternoon when we got back, so we had dinner and decided it was going to be an early night for all of us.

The next day, we went to Acadia National Park; some of the most beautiful scenery anywhere. We all had a good time, and we took some great pictures of Jeremy, Sara, Ana, and Sophie. I wish I could explain to you the look in Roger's eyes when he looks at his son and his family; it is like a person being given the most magnificent gift they could ever want. His love for them all is just wonderful to watch, and I look at them the same way as I look at all my children with a love bigger than can be told or expressed.

We were on our way south and heading for home we stopped in Augusta for dinner and then home; we were all glad to be home, we were exhausted, but after the girls went to bed, we sat around and talked. I love listening to Roger and Jeremy swap navy stories these two men are like two peas in a pod. They find all the same things funny, and they are both outrageous. We finally all went to bed. I was so ready to lay my tired body down, my husband had the look of sheer joy on his face. His son was sleeping under his roof; as far as he was concerned, all was right in his world.

While Sophie and the family are at our house, she asked me if I could make her Halloween costume for her; she wants to be the Queen of Hearts from Alice in Wonderland. I told her I would and measured her, and we looked at patterns and fabric. I told her I would have it there on time. We took them all to Portland to see the lighthouses that are there, had lunch out, and had fun. Then we had a day of sightseeing around our area and then we asked Cheryl to come to dinner, I knew she and Jeremy would get along she was in the navy too, and she was stationed in Hawaii too; that is where Jeremy spent four of his six years in the navy. They had a lot to talk about, and we had a lovely evening; everyone seemed to enjoy themselves. Roger enjoys it when she is included in the things we do with family and holidays. Jeremy and his family were late leaving because of the weather; their flight kept getting canceled. Finally after two or three days, we had to take them to New Hampshire to catch a flight in Manchester, which is the only way they could get home to Knoxville, and it was time for the girls to go back to school. We got them there on time even though the weather was bad, and they made it and called when they got home.

September is an interesting month in Maine; sometimes it will be cold early, and sometimes it is hot, well hot for Maine, but usually the weather is changing, and it is rainy and cool, and the leaves start to change. Roger and I took time to go to the white mountains in New Hampshire, we thought we might spend the night, but we had not made reservations, so we drove back home late at night and enjoyed the drive. He took me other places during September and October, and we enjoyed our time prowling around and him showing me more things I had not seen, and we revisited Five Islands Harbor where he proposed again and gave me my engagement ring. While he was working, I was busy sewing Sophie's costume. It turned out great, and Sara sent us wonderful pictures of her wearing it on Halloween. We also got pictures of Ana all dressed up too.

So now, it is November, and I had to get ready for Thanksgiving. That means it's time to put the blankets on the bed, do my usual fall housekeeping, and put the winter clothes out and ready and store the summer things until late spring, like June. Roger would be working on Thanksgiving because it is a Thursday, and like when he was in the navy, he will not take off so the people with families would be able to be off. I did not mind because on Saturday the twenty-fourth is my birthday, and he will be home.

I started cooking desserts on Friday for Thanksgiving. I prepared a lemon meringue pie for Roger and a carrot cake for me. People think I do not know what dessert is because my favorites are sweet potato pie and carrot cake; they say my desserts are made from vegetables. I like vegetables. We celebrated my birthday on Saturday, going out to dinner, and then on Sunday, I finished up our Thanksgiving dinner.

December in Maine is cold and usually snow on the ground, but it makes the Christmas decorations look fabulous. I enjoy the decorating part always have. I loved helping my mom decorate when she was alive; we had so much fun. I always start with the tree, and if I'm not going south before Christmas to take cookies and candy, I try to mail them to my children and grandchildren. Then I make sure all the presents are in the mail and on time just like I did last year, but next year, I will be down there in Tennessee and can go to Charleston to see the rest of them. Come on, 2013; I am ready to get this show on the road.

Chapter 31

It is now 2013, and we are hurrying to get the house ready to put on the market so we can sell it. Right after the new year, we started with little things we wanted to change and fix. We started on the half bath downstairs and the kitchen; we ordered the floors and countertops for both rooms. I removed the wallpaper in both rooms and painted them before the floors came, and we had the countertops installed. Then I cleaned the grout on the backsplash in the kitchen, and it looked like new when I finished it.

Roger asked Cheryl to come over and get anything of her mother's we were not taking to Oak Ridge with us, and she did, and that helped move some of the things out. I wanted her to have whatever she wanted that Roger was not wanting to keep. I know that was the way I felt about our mother's things; in fact, when we seven siblings met at my mother's house the boys told Bonnie, Evelyn, and myself we were Mama's girls; we should get whatever we wanted first and they would take what was left. I wanted Cheryl to do the same thing; you know the old saying, "Do unto others as you want them to do unto you!" I felt we still had things to go there were pieces that we did not want and things we did not have room for. I called the Restore, and they came and got what they could in three trips. That pared it down nicely, and there are things I had to pack now to get it out of the house, so we rented an indoor space for our boxes.

Nobody had packed up the clothes in the basement, so my friend Jane came over and helped me pack it all up, and she, bless her, took it to the goodwill for me. She knew we were rushed to get things done and helped immensely.

The work was going fine, and we were progressing, but there were things I could not do. We had to have some tile repaired in the foyer the grout was loose and had to be redone. Roger called his stepson, Scott G, and he came up from Connecticut; he is a carpenter and a whole lot of other things, like a jack of all trades. He helped us and spent some time with his sister Cheryl that live across the river in another small town.

I do not think they think they are small, but where you come from where we did, it is small. What used to be villages in the northeast is now towns. Our small towns in the south become cities in a hurry, especially if they are close to military bases. In Goose Creek where I grew up at one time, we just about everyone, then the military grew, and it exploded into a city. It was already a city in 1961. We have an army depot, which is where my father worked. We have an air base, a naval yard, and a naval weapons station in the Charleston area. Now the naval yard work has moved to other places, the air base, weapons station, and the army depot are still there.

Scott G arrived in good time; he is such a nice, friendly guy. I enjoyed working with him. He replaced the floors in the family room, which entailed removing the wood burning stove, the brick platform, and the carpet. Roger helped with some of this when he was not working. We also decided to take the carpet off the stairs, so we bought stair treads, and I sanded them and stained them to the color of our wood floors three times; it made the entrance to the house look grand.

Scott G redid the brick porch coming into the foyer of the family room where a half bath and laundry room are. Then we or I should say I did a lot of painting. I did have help though our real estate agent's ex-husband had done some handyman work outside, so Roger hired him again to help me paint. You very rarely will see Roger with a paintbrush in his hand; he does not like to paint. I think it is a navy thing because if it does not move in the navy, you paint it, but in his case, they painted and repainted airplanes all the time.

The boys came for a few weeks, and it was so nice to see them and spend time with them, and again, Chelsea could not come she was doing cheerleading, and they were practicing all the time and she did not like to miss that. She enjoyed it so much, and from all accounts, she was good at it. She is a tiny little thing. I miss her more than I can say. It's been very hard on me to let go of these children and let their parents raise them because when they lived with me. I saw to what they needed and made sure they were okay, and their homework done. If I had never been in that position, I would not feel this way and after the parents go in a different direction in life; they seem to forget the bond I had with their children.

All the painting was done except Roger's office; it had two desk and four bookcases loaded down with stuff like extra computer parts obsolete parts and books and more books and pictures. I packed everything on his shelves while he was at work, and he unhooked his equipment. Now it is hot, and I had to paint, UGH. So I carried on and got it done. I do not think there was a dry spot on my body when I stopped painting; the only thing left was behind one of his desk, and I could not move it. When I went to bed that night, I thought to myself, *Girl, you are crazy. All you had to do was roll this air conditioner into that room and you would have been cool.* Now I think about that.

It was in late July, early August, and Cathy, our realtor, came to take pictures of the house and put it on the market. The pictures showed it so well, and it looked great. I had taken every care to take our personal life out of the house so others could imagine themselves living there. The next day, I went shopping when Cathy called me and asked if I had mowed the grass yet, and I told her no and asked why she said, "I have three people that want to come and see it tomorrow." Trust me, I went home and mowed the grass right then. We had a buyer the next day for the price we wanted; we were elated. Now we set up a closing date and arranged for moving company to take our things to Tennessee. It was rush and go from then on getting everything packed that I wanted to pack myself, and then we had things to sell we were not keeping like lawnmowers, snow machines, generator, and a whole shed of things we would not need. That done, I went to work on the garage. Roger is a handyman, and he keeps things for a rainy day, and he has lots of things. I bought eighteen gallons, containers, and filled them with jars of nuts, bolts, screws, and nails. All kinds of paraphernalia he has almost every kind of hand tool you could think of plus real tall toolboxes full of tools.

We were down to the last day before the movers came getting everything ready. Thank goodness, Jane came over and helped Roger while I got the people from church to help me move the things. We had in storage back to the house for the movers to take. We rented an apartment for three weeks, but Jane was going to see her grandchildren in Utah, so she told us to stay at her house. We did and enjoyed our stay until the last day when they had Roger's retirement party. The next day, we left Jane's and was on our way to Tennessee. Whew what a lot of work we had done, so we took our time getting to our new home. Our furniture was already there; the movers had delivered everything and Jeremy was there to take delivery and to tell them what room each piece of furniture went to and what wall to put it on. That was a lot of help; we were able to make our bed and take a shower with the fresh linens I brought with us. So all we had to do was go to dinner somewhere and come back and take a shower and go to bed. We were ready to go to sleep in our new house in our bed; the days of travel had worn us out.

Tennessee here we are with lots to do again, we had so much unpacking to do, groceries to buy, and things to find like dishes and pots and pans, so I could cook again. We were settling in all over again, and I told Roger I never want to move again it is hard work. When I moved to Maine, it was not so bad. I packed my things, and they were ready to go I left all the furniture and things for Lori. She had to move the furniture, dishes, and linens when she moved at the end of the month after I got married. Roger had lived in his house for twenty-four years, and it was full as I have stated before. Well, now I am done I had lived in my house in Goose Creek for thirty-three years. I do not like to move.

We stayed busy with unpacking. Bonnie and Evelyn came to help us unpack, and we enjoyed that. We were also going to Ana and Sophie's soccer games with Dave and Marylee, Roger was enjoying being a grandpa up close, and I was loving it too. Getting to know the girls and spending time with them, I could hardly wait for the holidays. We are going to Charleston to see our families and then back to Oak Ridge to celebrate with the families here.

We ran into a couple of bumps in the road early on. I thought I was having a heart attack, but when they finished all the test, they decided it was stress. I cannot, for the life of me, imagine why it was stress. What stress? Oh my goodness, when boxes of things are out of place and sitting in the middle of the floor, they drive me crazy so there is your stress. Take a deep breath and get on with putting it up so the stress will go away—that is what I did.

Our friend Jane came to visit; well, she met us in Charleston, and we went sightseeing there. We took her to the ocean. Seeing the ocean was not a big deal for her see lives in Brunswick, Maine, but wading in the water in October was, it was still warm in October. We also took her to see the Angel Oak Tree. It is about 1,500 years old and glorious. I have a picture of it with the genealogy of JESUS. It starts at Adam at the root and JESUS is at the top; it hangs over our bed. When we came back to Oak Ridge, Jane went to visit her uncle over by Maryville. Her family was one of the original Tipton's that lived in Cades Cove, Tennessee. We enjoyed her visit; we love her very much, and she is a lot of fun.

Our holidays started with Halloween that year. Jeremy and Sara go all out for Halloween. They put up tables in their cul-de-sac and serve hot chocolate and spiced apple cider to all the people that come by in addition to candy and the dozens of cookies Marylee and I made. People come from all over to trick or treat at their house. We sat in lawn chairs between visits and drank apple cider when we were not serving other people. They were all nice and appreciative. We had a lot of fun watching all the children that were dressed up. I made Sophie and Ana's outfits Sophie was Harley Quinn from Batman and Ana was the Tennessee Volunteers monster. They were too cute. Sara told Roger he could go trick-or-treating with the girls and he pulled Jeremy aside and said, "I have never done this with children what do I do?" Jeremy took pity on him and went with him.

Roger later told me when they came to the first house he asked Jeremy if he was supposed to go with them to the door, and Jeremy laughed said to him, "You really have never done this before have you?"

And Roger replied, "No, I was raising other people's teenagers and young adults when I was in the navy for thirty years." With Halloween over, it was time for cooler weather and thinking of Thanksgiving and Christmas.

This was our first thanksgiving in Tennessee; we were able to go home for a visit before Thanksgiving and that was so nice. I got to see my family and Roger was able to catch up with some of his. It is a six- to six-and-a-half-hour trip to Evelyn's house she invited us to come and stay with her. We enjoy being with her and Otto we like the same things. Well, except Otto likes to play golf and Roger stopped playing when he got out of the navy. He went back to school to get a second degree. With most things, we are on the same page.

We were invited to Dave and Marylee's house for Thanksgiving dinner, and we had a wonderful time; however, I never go empty-handed, I always carry a salad or a dessert. This time, I carried both. We feasted like king and queens; we had dinner and then dessert with coffee afterward. They are so comfortable to be around, and they make everyone feel welcome to their home. Friday, Sara, Marylee, and I did a little shopping on Black Friday, which is something I don't usually want to do, but it was fun.

Now is the time to get busy for Christmas. I made stockings to hang on the mantle for me and Roger while we were still in Maine, so I made some for Jeremy, Sara, and the girls and for Nathan. I am going to get him, so he can spend Christmas with me. I miss having him for Christmas when I was in Maine. I don't care if I have to drive six and a half hours twice to get him for two weeks. To me as his MaMa, it is worth it. I love all my grandchildren, but he was my baby for a long time. He was the youngest from 2002 until I met Ana and Sophie in 2010. Then Nathan moved over because now Sophie is the youngest. I loved those girls even before I met them looking at pictures of them. They reminded me of Evelyn and me when we were young girls.

We figured out Christmas easily. Jeremy and family got up and had Christmas at their house and then they went to Dave and

Marylee's just like they always do. Then in the afternoon, they came to our house for their Christmas with us. We like this plan simply fine. Roger and I do not like to get up early. We never went to bed early in Maine because he got off so late had to drive home, and then we would go to bed so we slept late—well, until nine o'clock. When the children came to our house, we had present opening and fun, then Dave and Marylee, and Sara's sister Mo and her boyfriend came too because during the day, I was cooking Christmas dinner, and we ate around six o'clock. Nathan and the girls have a lot of fun too, swapping presents and being goofy the way kids are.

Chapter 32

In this chapter, I am going to fill you in on some of the things we have learned about our new family we have acquired; hold on tight to you seat these things are amazing.

Back in 1989, when my mom told me that my son had come to her house and that his name was Jeremy, I notified Roger so he would know what was going on. I gave him all the information I had. I joined the Triad group; they helped parents by telling them where and how to look for their grown children that had been given up for adoption. So I searched the records of the courthouse in Charleston for the records of his adoption by the attorney's name. There were several adoptions, and I made a list of them all after Jeremy was born. I wrote down the case number the parents' names and the boy's names and where they came from. I never used the information because we had a horrible hurricane in September that year, and all the records had to be moved because of the flooding and devastation downtown. So I packed away all the information I had and left it; years later, when I was packing my thing to move to Maine when I got married, I uncovered my books and records; when I opened it right there, in black and white was Jeremy's parents' names and his name. I had the information all the time from 1989, and I found it again in 2012. I realized GOD was not ready, then it had to be when HE was ready.

When Jeremy was a teenager, he lived in a small town in Connecticut; he used to ride his bike by this bridge where all the kids hung out after school. Roger and Irene, his first wife, used to cross that bridge just about every Friday and see the kids out there; they were going to her sister's house who was ill at the time. After all this time, the things we did not have a clue about the times we could have run into him. I looked at every little redheaded boy with green eyes when he was growing up, hoping to see him someday. But he had white blond hair and blue eyes.

We went to soccer games all the time and the summer of 2014. Ana was going to Washington, DC, for a conference for TSA (Technology Student Association). She was participating in some of the challenges, and while there she was going to lay a wreath on the Tomb of the Unknown Soldier. They were asked to write a paper on why they should be chosen to have this honor, and she won along with a male classmate. This was something we wanted to see, so we asked Sara, and she was glad to have us, and we stayed in the same hotel as she and Sophie did. Ana stayed with the school group. Sophie found a new friend at this swank hotel we stayed in with a rooftop bar and pool and in the afternoons she and her Sara went up there. This is the place a lot of the millennials hang out, and the young people did not want to get their hair and makeup messed up. When Sophie and her friend got in the pool, they pretty much cleared it out. Sophie was seven, and so was her friend. They had no clue what they were doing, but it was funny.

The morning that we went to the Tomb of the Unknown Soldier, the weather was nice, and we got to watch the guards and a changing of the guards. Jeremy explained to Ana about how to walk in, unison with the guard leading her classmate and herself to the wreath. All I could do was hold my breath, and then I looked at my husband, and he had tears running down his face he was so proud it is a wonder he could even stand there. After it was over and they had finished, he told me, "I never thought I would have grandchildren, and now for this to happen and today of all days, the day I turn sixty-five years old is such a blessing." So now I cried too; it was very moving and awe-inspiring, and the best birthday present he could imagine.

The second year we were here in Tennessee, Ana and Sophie came over to decorate the Christmas tree; they were having fun in the living room and Jeremy, Sara, Roger, and I were at the kitchen table drinking coffee when all of a sudden, Sophie came running into the kitchen with a glass bird ornament in her hand, and she asked me, "Why does this bird have my name on it with these numbers on it?"

I told her that was her name, but in this case, it was her grandpa's mother's name. She was a Sophie too. She looked at me and exclaimed, "She was named after me?" That is when we knew that nothing happens in Sophie's life unless it happened after she was born.

After I moved to Tennessee, I taught Sophie to sew, and she learned fast and did amazing work for her age. She started middle school and got involved in the 4-H Club and had fun the first year and did well at all she participated in. The next year, she decided to make a beautiful dress and enter the Queen contest. I watched over her as she made the dress, and she did amazing, and she also won the crown. After that, she entered the fair and won a blue ribbon for the things she made. The next year, she made a stunning dress and wore it when she crowned the new queen. We went to Disney, and she made a leather coat and a vest so she could be the scarlet witch and entered all this in the fair and won Blue ribbons again. She made a dress with fabric that her grandma Cindy sent her. It was fabric that her grandfather Dick had bought for her grandmother Cindy from overseas; it was old and beautiful, and it also made a gorgeous dress.

We went to Disney or Universal every year with Jeremy and family, and with Nathan when we went in the summertime, they have different fall and spring breaks at school. Sometimes we went then, and Nathan was still in school. So when we went in the summer, he went with us.

The year 2017 was a busy year. Lori was having a little girl in June and before that Wesley, Chelsea and Hunter were graduating from high school. Wesley came to stay with us the Christmas of 2016, so I could take him to have his senior pictures made, we also ordered his class ring. I got busy making baby clothes—a nursery ensemble with bumper pads, sheets, a matching quilt, pillow, and diaper stacker. Then I made crib pads, lap pads, burp pads, I covered all the bases. I tried to remember everything she would need, then I had her a shower and invited the family. By the time it was over, she had everything. I took her a crib and a stroller too.

I went back home because I had to go to Harvest, Alabama, where Wesley was living with his father and family for his graduation. Then back to my house to repack and get ready to go back to Charleston for Kyrah's birth and Chelsea's graduation. Wesley drove over from Alabama and is going with us to his mom's; we were about twenty minutes out when Lori called me from the hospital and said, "Mom, I can't wait for you to get here the baby is coming now." I told her, "Go ahead." I would be there when she was done. I guess because I was with her when she had the boys; she thought I should be there this time too, but that was okay with me I got to hold a beautiful baby girl when I got there, and my baby (Lori) was doing fine. We then went to Chelsea's graduation, another milestone for one of my grands and me.

We are so lucky our son and his family love us; you cannot imagine what it is like when they come over, come in the house, and make themselves at home sometimes we laugh when they leave, and sometimes, we want to weep because we know how blessed we are.

I am sure the years to come will get more interesting as time goes on; the grandchildren will see to that. I look forward to what is to come. I know the LORD is always with me and watching over me, my husband, and my children and grandchildren wherever they go and whatever they choose to do with their lives.

So now I have told you this wonderful true story. I hope you understand why I chose to name it *In God's Time* because GOD has a time and place for everything and HE works all things for the good of those who love HIM and are called according to HIS purpose (Rom. 8:28).

The last thought I want to leave you with is, when you love the LORD GOD and give your life to HIM, HE will give you the desires of your heart. In my case, a desire I had not even conceived, to be with Roger again, loving him as I always did, and the both of us having Jeremy and his family in our lives, what a loving GOD we have. Always remember, you cannot outgive GOD.

The end.

About the Author

Betty B. Hilton was fourteen when she met her first love; it was love at first sight for both of them. She never stopped loving this young man who was sixteen at the time. They were inseparable, and they spent as much time together as possible.

Things changed, and then they were having a baby, very scary for a fifteen- and seventeen-year-old. That is when Betty's world fell apart. We were separated for the next forty-three years.

Betty later married a wonderful man and had two fabulous children, a boy and a girl. They filled her life for a long time with happiness and hope. Betty lost her husband after twenty-eight years and nine months. Once more, Betty's life was devastated.

When you give your life to the Lord and let Him run it, anything is possible, or so Betty found out.

Printed in the USA
CPSIA information can be obtained
at www.ICGtesting.com
CBHW031617011124
16780CB00045B/532